A
Philanthropic
Covenant
with Black America

A Philanthropic Covenant with Black America

Edited by
Rodney M. Jackson

Introduction by
Tavis Smiley

Afterword by
Emmett D. Carson

WILEY
John Wiley & Sons, Inc.

Published by John Wiley & Sons, Inc., Hoboken, New Jersey.
Published simultaneously in Canada.

No part of this publication may be reproduced, stored in a retrieval system, or transmitted in any form or by any means, electronic, mechanical, photocopying, recording, scanning, or otherwise, except as permitted under Section 107 or 108 of the 1976 United States Copyright Act, without either the prior written permission of the Publisher, or authorization through payment of the appropriate per-copy fee to the Copyright Clearance Center, Inc., 222 Rosewood Drive, Danvers, MA 01923, 978-750-8400, fax 978-646-8600, or on the web at www.copyright.com. Requests to the Publisher for permission should be addressed to the Permissions Department, John Wiley & Sons, Inc., 111 River Street, Hoboken, NJ 07030, 201-748-6011, fax 201-748-6008, or online at http://www.wiley.com/go/permissions.

Limit of Liability/Disclaimer of Warranty: While the publisher and author have used their best efforts in preparing this book, they make no representations or warranties with respect to the accuracy or completeness of the contents of this book and specifically disclaim any implied warranties of merchantability or fitness for a particular purpose. No warranty may be created or extended by sales representatives or written sales materials. The advice and strategies contained herein may not be suitable for your situation. You should consult with a professional where appropriate. Neither the publisher nor author shall be liable for any loss of profit or any other commercial damages, including but not limited to special, incidental, consequential, or other damages.

For general information on our other products and services, or technical support, please contact our Customer Care Department within the United States at 800-762-2974, outside the United States at 317-572-3993 or fax 317-572-4002.

Wiley also publishes its books in a variety of electronic formats. Some content that appears in print may not be available in electronic books. For more information about Wiley products, visit our Web site at http://www.wiley.com.

Library of Congress Cataloging-in-Publication Data

A philanthropic covenant with Black America / edited by Rodney M. Jackson ; introduction by Tavis Smiley.
    p. cm.
  Includes bibliographical references and index.
  ISBN 978-0-470-39792-3 (cloth)
  1. African Americans—Charities.   2. African Americans—Charitable contributions.
3. Community development—United States.   I. Jackson, Rodney M.
  HV3181.P45 2009
  361.7'608996073—dc22

                                         2009001908

Printed in the United States of America

10 9 8 7 6 5 4 3 2 1

Contents

Contents

Contents

Contents

Contents

Contents

Foreword

In 2006 I had the privilege and honor to spearhead the creation of *The Covenant with Black America*, one of the most phenomenal publishing and social accomplishments of this decade. *The Covenant* reached #1 on the best-seller lists of the *New York Times Book Review*, the *Washington Post*, the *Los Angeles Times*, *USA Today*, Barnes and Noble, and Borders. It also became the basis for nationwide civic action as communities mobilized to make *The Covenant* a living, breathing document.

A year later, *The Covenant* was followed by *The Covenant in Action*, which chronicled the steps black people have taken in response to the challenges set forth in *The Covenant*. One of the many innovative projects reported in the second volume was an undertaking by the National Center for Black Philanthropy, Inc. (NCBP), located in Washington, D.C., to develop what they called *A Philanthropic Covenant with Black America*.

Originally conceived as a brief volume for their 2007 national conference, *A Philanthropic Covenant* blossomed into the full-length book you are holding now. I am very pleased to note that several of my colleagues who were instrumental in producing *The Covenant* have also played key roles as contributing authors in *A Philanthropic Covenant*. Their involvement has helped to make a smooth transition from one book to the other.

My abiding friend Dr. Cornel West made an astute observation when he said, "The crisis in Black America is threefold . . . economic, political, and spiritual." While the election of President Barack Obama clearly shows that America has come a long way in its political development, we must not lose sight of the large numbers of African Americans who have yet to catch up with this progress. Philanthropy—the giving of time, talents, and treasure—is already an important strategy in assisting black communities. But it can become even more effective when individuals are giving of *their own* time, talents, and treasure in support of other African Americans.

This is what *A Philanthropic Covenant with Black America* is really about and why it deserves your attention. When the hearts and minds of black people are motivated and mobilized, there is no problem we can't solve. Dr. Martin Luther King said, ". . . we've got to strengthen black institutions [and] begin the process of building a greater economic base." Philanthropy—black philanthropy—can help accomplish both.

I congratulate the National Center for Black Philanthropy on its achievements with *A Philanthropic Covenant*, and I trust you, the reader, will give it the same generous level of thought and consideration that you accorded to *The Covenant*. It is an important action plan for achieving not only civil rights, but "silver" rights.

Finally, please look for the third volume in *The Covenant* series, *Accountable: Making America as Good as Its Promise*, by Tavis Smiley with Stephanie Robinson.

Tavis Smiley

Acknowledgments

We want to take this opportunity to acknowledge the many individuals whose time, talents, and treasure made this book possible. First, we want to thank Tavis Smiley for bringing us his brilliant, *The Covenant with Black America*, which set the stage upon which this volume was built. We also thank Tavis for his unhesitating support and encouragement when we first announced the book, for featuring it in *The Covenant in Action*, and for providing the Foreword to this volume.

We also thank our good friend, colleague, and board member emeritus, Dr. Emmett D. Carson, for providing the thoughtful Afterword to this book. All of us who are involved in African-American philanthropy and volunteerism owe Dr. Carson a huge debt of gratitude for his many years of leadership and scholarship in these areas. It was only appropriate to have allowed him to have the last word.

Acknowledgments

Next, we thank all the authors—Angela Glover Blackwell, Birgit Smith Burton, Kermit "K.C." Burton, Charisse Carney-Nunes, Jeannette Davis-Loeb, Carol Brunson Day, Rodney M. Jackson, Stephanie R. Robinson, Judith Gordon Samuel, Harold Dean Trulear, and Sherece Y. West—who so brilliantly crafted the ideas that will henceforth be known as *A Philanthropic Covenant with Black America*. It is our fervent hope that this book will make a worthy companion to Tavis Smiley's *The Covenant*. We send a special note of thanks to our president and CEO, Mr. Jackson, for having conceived of the idea of the Philanthropic Covenant and edited the volume.

We also want to thank Dr. L. Lauretta Baugh for her review and insights on portions of the text; Norma Denise Mitchem for her unwavering support and encouragement throughout the development of this book; Penland L. Woods, volunteer extraordinaire, for sharing her first-hand experiences and insights; Allan R. Clyde for his editorial assistance in the initial development of the book; the publisher, John Wiley & Sons, and our editor, Judith Howarth, for their unswerving belief in this book and their saint-like patience with its development.

We thank the Annie E. Casey Foundation and former Senior Program Director, K.C. Burton, for having provided the grant that allowed us to pursue this book.

The National Center for Black Philanthropy, Inc.
Samuel L. Gough, C.F.R.E., Chair, Board of Directors

Introduction

Anyone not poor enough to receive is rich enough to give.
—Fredrick E. Jordan, African-American
Businessman and Philanthropist

At the beginning of his introduction to *The Covenant with Black America*, Tavis Smiley asked an intriguing question: Why a Covenant with Black America? Tavis answered his question, in part, with an anecdote taken from the life of the late civil rights leader, A. Philip Randolph, which concluded with an admonition from then-president Franklin Delano Roosevelt about the importance of "organizing and mobilizing" to bring about social change.

It is both fair and appropriate to ask the same question about this book: Why a *Philanthropic* Covenant with Black America? To answer this question, we must briefly examine the concept of philanthropy and its role in the history of African Americans.

The word *philanthropy* does not easily roll off the tongue, nor does its correct definition immediately come to mind. To many

Introduction

Americans, *philanthropy* conjures up an ethereal and mysterious world in which the wealthy give money to charity, motivated primarily by the tax write-offs they receive. It is a world dominated, mostly, by very wealthy whites; although, a few wealthy African Americans are seen as also being members of this exclusive club. (Oprah Winfrey and Bill Cosby immediately come to mind.) And most African Americans are viewed as recipients rather than givers of philanthropy.

In 2009 we are beginning to understand that this is more of a caricature of philanthropy than a true reflection (though some might argue otherwise). Thanks to the research of scholars like Ambassador James A. Joseph and Dr. Emmett D. Carson, we now know that the "impulse for philanthropy," as Ambassador Joseph put it, is not the exclusive province either of one race or one economic class. The philanthropic impulse can also be found by examining the history and current practice of communities of color: black, Latino, and Native American, as well as Asian American and Pacific Islanders.

Among African Americans, philanthropy is more commonly referred to as "giving back." Philanthropy, or giving back, has been an integral part of black U.S. history and can be traced back to African culture and values that survived the Middle Passage and chattel slavery. "Historically," according to Dr. Carson, "black philanthropy has been a survival mechanism through which African American people directed their money, time and goods to lift up and advance the myriad interests of African-American people."[1] Black philanthropy, "synonymous with African-American survival and perseverance,"[2] became the very embodiment of the contribution of "time, talent and treasure" that benefited blacks and non-blacks alike.

In 1967 Dr. Martin Luther King, Jr. challenged African Americans to "develop a kind of dangerous unselfishness." Black philanthropy may be unselfish, but it is hardly dangerous; not dangerous in a literal sense—although there were times in black history when the practice of philanthropy by African Americans was in fact dangerous—it is used here in the sense of one of its synonyms, "risky."

The tenacious, ongoing problems in the black community, so well documented in *The Covenant,* that seem so resistant to change, will require a full court press, if they are ever to be solved. This means being intentional and strategic in the use of our time and talent, and willing to take risks with our treasure. It has been said many times that we cannot expect anyone else to rescue us. Improving black communities, ultimately, is something we have to do for ourselves by committing our time, talent, and treasure in purposeful, strategic ways.

A Philanthropic Covenant with Black America invites all those who believe in "giving back," "leaving no one behind," or "each one reaching one" to recommit to bringing about change in black communities. This book shows that everyone has a role to play. Grantmakers, who are particularly averse to taking risks, are challenged to do just that. The need in black communities for the expertise of fundraising professionals, particularly African Americans, has never been more urgent. African American religious congregations are challenged to "revisit their philosophy and theology of giving to black communities." Black youth should be encouraged to learn the value of giving, rather than receiving. Civic engagement is a powerful strategy for strengthening and developing cohesion in black communities. Black families, far from being the poster children for dysfunction, can be the cornerstones for black community renewal. Black communities can join together and begin planning in advance to reduce the effects of natural disasters. And volunteers, particularly African Americans, can be integral parts of all the aforementioned.

Introduction

People and institutions that commit to actions that strengthen black communities can be said to be carrying out "Covenant Commitments."

Finally, in order to ensure that adequate funding is available for these efforts, and in the spirit of self-help that has characterized black philanthropy for 200 years, we ask your consideration of a major $100 million "Covenant Fund for Black Communities."

Making Covenant Commitments to strengthen black communities *and following through on them* will indeed require the kind of "dangerous unselfishness" that Dr. King spoke of. Ironically, this was the phrase that Dr. King used in his famous, "I Have Seen the Promised Land," speech in Memphis the evening before he was assassinated. In the same speech, he also said, "Be concerned about your brother. You may not be on strike. But either we go up together, or we go down together."

What was true then is equally true now. Despite the current economic crisis (or maybe because of it), history may have handed us an unprecedented opportunity to finish the job of bringing equal opportunity to *all* African Americans. Everyone concerned with progress in the black community should read this book and then answer this question: Have you made your Covenant Commitment today? The future of our people in America may depend upon your answer.

Rodney M. Jackson

Notes

1. Emmett D. Carson, Ph.D., "African American Philanthropy at the Crossroads." In *At the Crossroads: The Proceedings of the First National Conference on Black Philanthropy*, ed. Rodney M. Jackson (Oakton, VA: The Corporation for Philanthropy, 1998), p. 10.
2. Ibid.

Chapter 1

Empowering the African American Community through Strategic Grantmaking

Angela Glover Blackwell
Founder and CEO, PolicyLink, Oakland, CA

Facts

- More than 72,000 foundations in the United States were responsible for $42.9 billion in giving in 2007, according to the Foundation Center, a research organization focused on philanthropy. Adjusted for inflation, grant dollars have more than doubled since 1997.[1]

The author gratefully acknowledges the writing contributions of Katrin Sirje Kärk, former PolicyLink senior writer, and Fran Smith, PolicyLink senior communications consultant; and for her insight on many of the climate change implications this chapter contains, Danielle Deane, program officer, Environment, The William and Flora Hewlett Foundation.

- A Foundation Center analysis of grants of $10,000 or more awarded by a national sample of large foundations found that 7 percent of dollars were designated explicitly for racial and ethnic minorities, including 1.5 percent for African Americans and 1.2 percent for Latinos.[2]
- Twelve percent of grants by large independent foundations, but only 7.7 percent of grant dollars, went to minority-led organizations in 2004, according to a study by the Greenlining Institute, a policy and advocacy organization. When a $535 million grant to the United Negro College Fund was excluded from the analysis, minority-led groups received only 3.6 percent of grant funding.[3]
- Foundation Center analyses show that almost 46 percent of grant dollars go to health and education. Fourteen percent go to human services, a broad category that includes criminal justice, food and nutrition, employment, housing, youth development, sports and recreation, and safety and disaster relief. Environment and animals receive 6 percent of grant funding.[4]
- In a 2007 study of giving by its members, Environmental Grantmakers Association reported that 42 percent of funding went to species and land protection. Climate and energy received 13 percent. Eight percent went to pollution and toxics, including 2.4 percent for environmental justice.[5]

From marquee foundations dispensing the fortunes of corporate titans, to family foundations supporting causes close to a founder's heart, to community foundations striving to make a difference at home, the philanthropic sector offers vast resources to tackle the world's most pressing problems. But these resources have limits, and like government budgeting, foundation giving raises hard questions: Which organizations, issues,

and constituencies should receive grants and why? Who benefits? Who decides?

At the 2007 conference of the Council on Foundations, an
overflow crowd participated in a discussion of the Covenant with
Black America. Philanthropy leaders showed strong interest in
the Covenant agenda and their role in advancing it. And they
should.

Foundation investment can have a profound impact on struggling and disconnected populations. While the robust philanthropic sector should not serve as an excuse for the government
to abdicate responsibility for social, economic, and environmental welfare, foundations can and must work with the public and
private sectors to promote opportunity for all. Yet foundations
have not fully risen to this challenge. Relatively few dollars reach
communities of color and African Americans, in particular. People of color make up one-third of the population of the United
States, but research by the Foundation Center shows that only
7 percent of grant support is designated specifically for racial
and ethnic minorities. A mere 1.5 percent is targeted to African
Americans.

This minimal funding is not for lack of foundation interest in the issues affecting African Americans. On the contrary:
while prestigious institutions such as universities, museums, sym-
phonies, and opera companies hold high-profile fundraising
galas and attract elite benefactors, foundations have a much
broader portfolio. As Foundation Center statistics show, more
than 70 percent of grants of more than $10,000 support work in
health, education, human services, youth development, public
affairs, community development, and civil rights—areas of great
concern to the black community.

But do organizations funded to do this work have strong
alliances with, or allegiance to, communities of color? Is this

question regularly asked by foundations as they review proposals? Foundations have not generally done a good job of identifying organizations rooted in the black community and other
communities of color and providing support at the levels required to achieve significant, sustainable impact. A Greenlining Institute study of domestic spending by 25 of the nation's
largest foundations found that minority-led organizations received 12 percent of grants in 2005 but only 8 percent of grant
dollars, an indication that nonprofits run by people of color
typically receive relatively small grants, if they receive funding
at all.[6]

Many foundations support an established roster of grantees
or concentrate on a narrow set of issue areas, making it difficult
for new constituencies and organizations without significant
connections to foundation professionals to step up from small
project-oriented grants to substantial funding. Certainly some
foundations seek out innovation and untested grantees, but
like all habits, long-standing grant practices prove challenging
to break. Achieving the goals of the Covenant with Black
America will require many well-run, well-resourced, dedicated
groups with staying power that are accountable to communities
of color.

What does it mean to be "accountable to communities of
color"? Is it sufficient that a person of color leads the organization? Must the majority of the staff be of color—and what about
racial diversity on the organization's board of directors? Would an
organization that focuses on a relevant issue—improving public
schools in cities, for example—be considered accountable given
the potential benefits of improved urban education for people
of color? Can an organization that does not have a voting membership ever be truly accountable?

These hard questions require finely nuanced answers that ultimately involve more art than science. Clearly an organization that focuses on building a more inclusive society, led by a person of color with a track record of service and struggle on issues affecting a particular racial or ethnic group or several communities of color, is a good example of accountability. This accountability is strengthened if people of color hold leadership positions on the staff and board. But is it also possible for that same organization, with the same agenda, and the same staff and board, to maintain a deep commitment and accountability to communities of color even without a leader of color?

True accountability is reflected in actions. It requires debating the issues with the affected communities. It means demonstrating a continuing commitment to improve conditions in communities of color and strengthen the authentic voice of people of color. Accountability exists when an organization steadfastly and reliably works with residents and/or leaders of color for the good of communities of color—even when such positions are not in vogue.

Creating an Equitable Portfolio

Unlike charitable organizations, devoted largely to providing for the short-term needs of individuals, many foundations use strategic philanthropy to determine how to allocate their money. Strategic grant making focuses on change and builds for the future. Ideally, strategic giving reflects and advances a foundation's core values and concerns.[7] Through strategic philanthropy, foundations can translate their *interest* in issues affecting people of color into *actions* to improve and strengthen communities of color.

The urgent need to confront climate change presents an exciting opportunity to use strategic grant making to build organizations committed to inclusion—and may lead to a case study of how to develop an equitable portfolio in any arena of concern to philanthropy.

As an emerging frontier for grant making, and one that will grow more critical in the years to come, climate change offers a way to be deliberate about inclusion from the outset. Strategic grant making can also help strengthen the connections between communities of color, environmental justice, and the mainstream environmental movement. In the popular culture, environmentalism has often been portrayed as the chic cause of affluent white Americans, but it is well documented that the poor are affected most by environmental problems. In fact, the grassroots environmental justice movement was born from the realization that low-income communities and communities of color often bear the brunt of air pollution, toxic dumping, dilapidated infrastructure, and undesirable public works sites such as sewage treatment plants and bus depots.

Although climate change threatens to cause catastrophic consequences that transcend race, class, and geography, the poor and people of color around the globe stand to suffer disproportionately. Weather fluctuations brought on by rampant consumption of energy, particularly in advanced industrial nations, are predicted to wreak havoc on the agriculture, infrastructure, and very survival of some of the world's poorest communities in Africa, Asia, and Latin America. In the United States, African Americans, Latinos, and other people of color once again will shoulder an unfair burden.

The Congressional Black Caucus Foundation conducted an exhaustive analysis of the impact of global warming on African Americans. The report—which is impressive in its scope and for the fact that the CBCF undertook this examination in 2004, well before celebrity activists took up the cause and Al Gore's galvanizing documentary, *An Inconvenient Truth,* effectively beat back the vestiges of skepticism about global warming—found that African Americans are less responsible for climate change because as a group, they create fewer greenhouse gases. But they are and will continue to be disproportionately affected by global warming.[8] According to the CBCF research, African Americans are more likely than whites to live in polluted communities; suffer from serious environment-related conditions such as asthma; and die in connection with hurricanes, floods, heat waves, and other extreme weather events. African Americans also are more vulnerable to the economic effects of global warming. The report noted that drought, sea level rise, and the higher temperatures associated with global warming may have particularly disruptive effects on agriculture, insurance, and buildings and infrastructure. "In general, economic transitions strike hardest at those without resources or savings to adapt," the CBCF said.

At no time in recent American history did the intersection of race, class, and government disregard become more shamefully evident than during Hurricane Katrina. In tandem with the forces of nature (in the form of the extreme storm that experts fear will occur more frequently as the earth's temperature changes) and policy neglect (in the form of inadequately maintained levees that failed to protect New Orleans from catastrophic flooding), Katrina exposed raw poverty and isolation to a shocked global public and offered a critical lesson to anyone committed to fighting climate change: It is necessary but not sufficient to focus on the environmental impacts. Philanthropists also must pay attention to the effects of global warming on people. Foundations need to invest in an advocacy infrastructure in communities throughout the United States that are vulnerable to the ravages of extreme weather, to ensure that future disasters do not disproportionately affect poor residents and people of color.

Like everyone else, foundations are scrambling to catch up with the growing threat of global warming. Research sponsored by several major foundations reached the chilling conclusion that if philanthropy, government, business, and individuals don't "act boldly in the next decade to prevent carbon lock-in, we could lose the fight against global warming." For example, coal plants under construction along with nonenvironmentally de-signed factories, homes, and commercial spaces built to last will emit carbon for years, even generations, to come.[9] Without strong, immediate action on energy efficiency, emissions will es-sentially snowball. Efficiency efforts will fall further and further behind, until mitigation may become impossible.

The danger in racing to respond is that equity will fall vic-tim to urgency and that unintended consequences of policies to combat global warming will reinforce existing disparities. How will new regulations, trading systems, or tax and incen-tive schemes play out in communities? If one city enacts green building requirements, for example, will affordable housing de-velopers raise prices on their units or abandon the area entirely for a more lax jurisdiction? How can people at all income levels take advantage of more fuel-efficient cars and energy-efficient appliances? Will carbon trading perpetuate environmental racism by encouraging plants that are already disproportionately located in low-income areas to pollute with greater impunity, knowing they can simply buy or trade their way out of reducing their own emissions?

Many policymakers are in the early stages of responding to climate change. They need to pay close attention to California's landmark global warming law, which includes a "no backsliding" provision to prevent "solutions" at the expense of communities of color. This type of protection should be at the center of other state and federal initiatives on carbon reduction, but in California and elsewhere implementation will be the true test. Without state commitment to spend adequate resources for monitoring, enforcement, and sanctions—and without vigilant, well-funded NGOs accountable to communities of color—disparities will likely persist.

Mobilizing Communities of Color

The philanthropic sector has cultivated some of the most creative and transformative economic, scientific, and social innovations—microlending, disease eradication, and community development financing, to name a few. Now foundations have an extraordinary moment to lead the United States and the global community in equitable, inclusive climate change policy and action. The tenfold increase in climate change and energy funding that several major foundations say will be necessary presents unprecedented opportunities for communities of color to be part of the solution to global warming.[10] Foundations must strike a balance between making critical and urgent grants to organizations already in the network and known in the field, on the one hand, and taking the time to seek out and support leaders and organizations that will pay attention to the impacts of global warming and mitigation and prevention strategies on communities of color, on the other.

Substantial grants typically go to large, well-established mainstream organizations, which have demonstrated the scientific, economic, legal, and political expertise to work on the complexities of climate change. Community-based, grassroots, and newer organizations (which are far more likely to serve and be led by African Americans and other people of color than mainstream national environmental organizations) often lack scientific and technical staff.

On the surface, this would seem to pose a dilemma for grant makers. Should they invest the time and resources to build a newer organization's scientific capacity, all the while falling behind in the race to cut carbon emissions? Or should they quickly get the money to established players who can hit the ground running? In fact, foundations can turn what looks like either/or into win-win.

Grant makers need African American communities and organizations as much as African Americans need foundation dollars. Where larger mainstream environmental groups can offer high-level technical expertise, organizations grounded in communities of color often excel at communications, advocacy, and organizing. Technology and business innovations are a first step toward mitigating global warming, but even the most promising strategies die without political momentum. As *Design to Win: Philanthropy's Role in the Fight Against Global Warming* noted, "policy reform is essential for tempering climate change."[11] Scientists and economists may be able to seed and develop technological advances and policy proposals, but community-based leaders can build public will and mobilize their community members to exert the political pressure necessary to enact reforms.

The most effective and sustainable grant making strategies bring together organizations with scientific capacity and organizations with advocacy expertise. Over the long term, foundations must also address diversity (or lack thereof) within the mainstream environmental movement and explore strategies to help organizations of color build their technical expertise—and help experts of color build their knowledge and gain a foothold in scientific and technological organizations.

Community-level environmental justice efforts may be off the radar of grant makers striving to achieve large-scale results that change state or national policy. But even though many community organizations may not have the current capacity to scale up, some victories and innovations at the local level would eventually progress to broad impact, if they have the funding and technical assistance to grow.

The philanthropy community also will miss a critical opportunity if foundations do not invest now in an advocacy infrastructure focused on the effects of global warming on people, particularly people of color. As Katrina made clear, it is not enough to focus solely on the environmental impacts of climate change. Foundations need to help the government and NGOs identify the regions most vulnerable to the consequences of climate change and to invest in strong advocacy sectors in those communities. Foundations must support and sustain community-based organizations working *now* to develop disaster relocation and recovery plans that address the needs of the low-income residents, people of color, and distressed neighborhoods.

Jobs for a Sustainable Future

Advocacy, organizing, and policy expertise are part of one critical sphere in which philanthropy can have tremendous impact; the other is the green jobs (sometimes called "green collar") sector that is expected to grow enormously with the need to implement climate change solutions. Equity and opportunity can—and must—be public policy goals as well as economic goals in the marathon effort to ensure an environmentally sustainable future. The integration of equitable policies with market realities can create a win–win situation for both the economy and communities of color.

A report commissioned by the United Nations Environment Program estimates that 2.25 million people worked in the renewable energy sector in 2006. To put that rough figure in perspective, total employment in the oil and gas sector was 2 million in 1999.[12] The UN estimates that the market for clean technology could reach $1.9 trillion by 2020. Juan Somavia, director general of the International Labor Organization, noted, "Investments in energy efficiency, clean energy technology and in renewable energy have enormous potential to create productive and decent work."[13]

But will communities most in need of economic development and sustainable-wage jobs have access to these new opportunities? There are no guarantees—and that creates a two-fold challenge. It is critical to leverage the potential for green-collar jobs, but environmental efforts to improve dirty industries run the risk of provoking a "green backlash" if reforms lead to job losses that are not offset by comparable jobs in growing sectors. Foundations can play a lead role in keeping these issues at the forefront of discussions about emerging clean industries. The growing green economy can play a pivotal role in the renewal of low-income communities and communities of color. The philanthropic community must support initiatives to ensure that policies and programs to deliver jobs and save the earth are well-funded and accountable to communities of color.

Building Power and Voice

Two promising initiatives are bringing together advocates from multiple sectors to build an inclusive, sustainable green economy. The Apollo Alliance is a broad coalition of labor unions, environmental organizations, business leaders, and urban and faith communities in support of a $300 billion, 10-year program to create three million clean energy jobs and reduce American dependence on foreign oil. Major national environmental groups, political leaders, and 23 international labor organizations have endorsed the coalition.

At the Clinton Global Initiative in 2007, Van Jones, cofounder and president of the Ella Baker Center, based in Oakland, California, announced the creation of Green for All. The campaign builds on the center's earlier green jobs advocacy to "secure $1 billion in funding for green-collar job training in order to lift 250,000 people out of poverty across the country."[14] Green for All will use national advocacy, technical assistance, and education to build public and legislative consensus to make sure that low-income workers, disadvantaged communities, and people of color can benefit from the opportunities created by green jobs.

These important efforts build on the work of environmental justice advocates who have fought for years for a healthier, more sustainable society for all. While advocates use various strategies and approaches to make change happen, many in the environmental justice movement share a common vision: to build community power and voice, not only to participate in the debate about our environmental future but also to set the terms and frame the issues in that debate.

The Environmental Justice Resource Center, at Clark Atlanta University, was formed in 1994 as a research and policy clearinghouse on race and the environment, land use planning, transportation equity, smart growth, and climate change. The center supports and trains students of color, professionals, and grassroots leaders to play vital roles in environmental research, policy formulation, and decision making. The director, Dr. Robert D. Bullard, has been an advocate for environmental justice since 1970, when neither environmentalists nor civil rights leaders recognized the ways in which our nation's environmental and industrial policies disproportionately harm communities of color.[15]

WE ACT for Environmental Justice (West Harlem Environmental Action, Inc.), a 20-year-old community-based organization in northern Manhattan, led by Peggy Shepard, was one of the first groups to effectively organize low-income people of color around issues of environmental health and sustainable development in their neighborhood.[16] The Deep South Center for Environmental Justice, run by Dr. Beverly Wright in New Orleans, has been a strong advocate for minority leadership along the Mississippi River corridor since 1992, and a leading voice for equitable, sustainable resettlement and reconstruction after Katrina.

The organizations and leaders cited above underscore the point about committed leaders with organizational capacity and accountability to communities of color. Van Jones, Robert Bullard, Beverly Wright, and Peggy Shepard are wonderful examples of visionary leaders who have been able to position themselves and their organizations to be ready and flexible so they can respond to the needs of low-income communities of color. There are many more leaders of color who are willing to act, but who need resources and support to become fully and sustainably engaged.

The need for immediate action on climate change presents a historic opportunity for philanthropy leaders to build comprehensive, inclusive grantmaking portfolios from the start. These portfolios will allow philanthropists not only to act on a global crisis but also to curb environmental racism and channel the benefits of environmental innovation to constituencies in greatest need.

But climate change marks only a starting point for equitable philanthropy. The strategies used to build inclusive portfolios to fight global warming can and must extend to grant making across the board—in education, health, justice, youth development, and every other issue that foundations care about. Foundations can fund advocacy that amplifies the political voice of African Americans and carries ideas through to lasting policy change that benefits everyone. The philanthropic community can support meetings that encourage organizations of all sizes and expertise to form partnerships and share knowledge. Foundations can nurture and sustain efforts to create equitable and sustainable communities, and education and workforce development programs that connect African Americans to emerging economic opportunities.

Foundations spend billions of dollars a year to help solve the problems facing our country. By making a firm commitment to inclusion, foundations can ensure that their massive investment empowers African Americans and other communities of color and brings new strengths to the tough challenges that face us all.

What Foundations Can Do

- Significantly expand the racial diversity on the boards and recruit more people of color who have demonstrated a deep commitment to and knowledge of historically excluded communities. Turning to search firms that developed the walkabouts and skills to reach deep into these networks will improve the chances of success.
- Use grant making—issue-based as well as core funding—to strengthen institutions that serve the interests of people of color and to support and groom leaders of color. These

investments pay off in unanticipated ways. For example, PolicyLink (the organization I lead, which has a diverse staff and board and works on a variety of issues that advance equity for all low-income communities and people of color, including African Americans), built a broad portfolio of policy expertise and a network of policy experts with generous core foundation support. PolicyLink was able to use these assets to make a valuable contribution to the black community when Tavis Smiley invited the organization to coordinate the *Covenant with Black America* book.

- Use a variety of institution-building investments; provide grants that help organizations build their communications capacity; strengthen their fundraising skills; improve management performance; engage in broad coalitions; build partnerships with entities that bring different skills, such as research institutions; and enable organizations to quickly move to new opportunities by having some flexible resources.

- Demonstrate commitment to inclusion from the start by assembling diverse advisors to develop funding strategies; hire consultants to do early assessments on the impacts of the issue area on different communities of color.

- Introduce organizations led by people of color to other funders; stay connected with these organizations and leaders by visiting their offices and developing supportive relationships; highlight these organizations in publications, on websites, and in presentations. These activities help build the leadership and visibility of groups that often work heroically but invisibly in their communities.

- Invest in a pipeline of experts of color in foundation issue areas by funding appropriate professors and departments at historically black colleges and universities and by establishing fellowships that increase diversity in academic institutions generally. Consider loan forgiveness programs, mentorships, and other activities that build a cadre of experts of color who can enter fields that lack diversity, especially policy.

• Evaluate foundation program officers based on criteria that reflect the foundation's desire to be more inclusive and build the capacity, visibility, and effectiveness of organizations that are accountable to communities of color and led by committed leaders of color.

• Although it's important to focus on results, take time to broaden the universe of actors. Take risks.

Notes

1. Foundation Center, *Foundation Yearbook: Facts and Figures on Private and Community Foundation,* 2008. Highlights available online at http://foundationcenter.org/gainknowledge/research/pdf/fy2008_ highlights.pdf.

2. http://foundationcenter.org/findfunders/statistics/pdf/08_fund_pop /2006/16_06.pdf.

3. Greenlining Institute, *Investing in a Diverse Democracy: Foundation Giving to Minority-Led Nonprofits,* 2006. Available online at www.green lining.org/resources/pdfs/InvestinginaDiverseDemocracyFoundation GivingtoMinorityLedNonprofits.pdf.

4. *Foundation Yearbook.*

5. Environmental Grantmakers Association, *Tracking the Field: A Rough Guide,* 2007.

6. The Greenlining Institute, *Funding the New Majority: Philanthropic Investment in Minority-Led Non Profits,* 2008. Available online at http://greenlining.org/sections/view/documents.

7. This definition is informed by the Putnam Community Investment Consulting statement on strategic philanthropy and particularly, the insights of Torie Osborn, Liberty Hill Foundation, and The Philanthropic Initiative, Inc. Further information available at www.putnamcic.com.

8. www.cbcfinc.org/pdf/Climate_Change.pdf.

9. California Environmental Associates, *Design to Win: Philanthropy's Role in the Fight Against Global Warming*, August 2007.

10. Ibid.

11. Ibid.

12. *Green Jobs: Toward Sustainable Work in a Low-Carbon World*, UNEP, ILO, ITUC Green Jobs Initiative. Preliminary report, December 2007. Available at www.unep.org/labour_environment/PDFs/Green-Jobs-Preliminary-Report-18-01-08.pdf.

13. International Labor Organization, "Climate change and the world of work: ILO Director-General outlines ILO role in new "Green Jobs Initiative," September 24, 2007. Available at www.ilo.org/global/About_the_ILO/Media_and_public_information/Feature_stories/lang–en/WCMS_084092/index.htm.

14. "Green for All: Ella Baker Center Launches a Bold New Initiative," 27 September 2007, available online at http://ellabakercenter.org/page.php?pageid=26&contentid=327.

15. See www.ejrc.cau.edu/.

16. See www.weact.org/Programs/SustainableDevelopment/tabid/190/Default.aspx.

Chapter 2

Philanthropy and Religion

Harold Dean Trulear, Ph.D.

*Associate Professor of Applied Theology, Howard University
School of Divinity, Washington, DC
Fellow, Center for Public Justice, Annapolis, MD
President, G.L.O.B.E. Ministries, Philadelphia, PA*

The State of Giving and Religion in the African American Community

Estimates vary concerning the amount and/or percentage of income that African Americans give to their houses of worship. In general, African American Protestants give larger a percentage of their household income to their congregations than do other Christians, save for conservative Protestants.[1] African Americans have a higher percentage of persons who give exclusively for religious purposes than any other ethnic group.[2] The press regularly reports figures estimating that 9 out of every 10 dollars of charitable giving in the African American community goes to religious institutions, while the White House Council of Economic Advisors puts the figure at about 60 percent.[3]

What these numbers do not show is that the African American faith community has a variety of relationships with philanthropy. Most apparent is the way in which African Americans financially support their religious institutions. Second, African Americans donate to religious charities whose work resonates with their own sense of values and implements programs consistent with their desires for advancement. Third, African American religious institutions donate to causes that are consistent with their vision for social change, but that require institutional infrastructure beyond their capacity. Finally, in the past generation, African American religious institutions have positioned themselves to receive philanthropic giving, both from individuals (including planned giving) and foundations.

In this rich mix of the history and opportunities for giving, religious organizations, especially congregations, must think strategically about their role in the enterprise of philanthropy and develop practical ways of engaging that enterprise. Religious organizations must look within their own traditions to determine the boundaries and parameters of their relationship with future philanthropic efforts. Those efforts should not be restricted to mobilizing existing resources for social programs that simply deliver social services, but should also advocate for those who receive supportive services.

This chapter will consider both the history of the various relationships of African American religious organizations to philanthropy and offer a vision for the future of that relationship. It argues specifically that African Americans have a rich history of charitable giving to and through their religious institutions, supporting both the delivery of social services and the promotion of social advocacy—what the African American religious community has called the prophetic tradition. In addition, that tradition is threatened by changes in contemporary culture and social arrangements that have not diminished giving per se, but rather have made giving more self-interested, less, and less prophetic. The chapter traces the contours of the prophetic giving tradition, and then notes challenges in each area, closing with a general call for a renewed commitment to African American prophetic philanthropy.

African American Support for Their Houses of Worship

However one looks at the data concerning African American religion and philanthropy, an important question remains: namely, when the money does come in, what type of religious activity does such charitable activity support?

The black church, along with the black family, stands as the oldest continuing institutions founded, led, and maintained by African Americans. From the first independent black congregations, Baptist and Methodist, called into being before the Revolutionary War up through the present, these houses of worship have depended primarily upon the personal donations of their memberships in order to begin, grow, and sustain their work.

As the spiritual face of the African American community, these congregations have provided the primary religious context for the health and well-being of the black community. At the same time, they have provided community and social services, voices of activism and protest, and tended to a diversity of issues such as education and economic development in their communities.[4]

A Philanthropic Covenant with Black America

The genius of such an institutional mission lies in its comprehensive approach to the needs and concerns of the black community as a whole. As demonstrated by the host of scholarship on the black church, congregations served their communities as stations of education, health care, economic development, political participation, and civic engagement. This reflects the historic connection of the black church in America to its African religious antecedents, where spirituality relates to all of life and there is no separation between the sacred and secular realms, as is characteristic of religion in the West. In addition racial conventions of slavery, segregation, and discrimination placed African American houses of worship, as the primary institutions with relative autonomy from white ownership, as the primary voice for social protest—the prophetic tradition—that spoke out against American racism in all its forms, and supported institutions designed to deal specifically with situations caused by racism and oppression. Therefore, to give to religious institutions is to invest in this prophetic tradition, but this means that if that tradition becomes marginalized, that even maintenance of giving levels to religious institutions in the black community results in a diminishing of prophetic African American philanthropy.

As such, historic giving by members to black churches supported work in all areas of social service and advocacy, reflecting a commitment to holistic community uplift. When public schools were either nonexistent or closed to blacks, local churches often filled the void. For a number of Baptist churches, the missionary offering (also called the "penny offering" in some churches) served to support local schooling efforts. The late George Kelsey, faculty mentor to Martin Luther King, Jr., at Morehouse College, once offered that "persons of my generation did not attend public schools. Our elementary school [in Griffin, Georgia,

22

circa 1920] was the local church of the pastor with the most education in the area. The Cabin Creek Baptist Association took up a regular offering for that pastor and his wife to teach us during the elementary school years. If you went to high school, it was at one of the residential academies connected with one of the area colleges." Benjamin Mays and other leaders of the area report similar experiences.[5]

When health care services were unavailable for the black community, black churches cared for the sick and their families. When few economic opportunities for blacks existed in many communities, the collective economic efforts of congregations represented a primary source of the circulation of dollars within the community. When counseling, crisis intervention, and mental health facilities did not (and do not) serve African American communities, black congregations served as therapeutic communities for mental health and wholeness.[6] Virtually any function filled in contemporary society by the nonprofit sector found its primary expression amongst blacks in their houses of worship. As such, the charitable giving that supported congregations also supported a myriad of social service needs as well. To the extent that African American congregations no longer serve such a comprehensive mission, one can argue that specific services that have become specialized within various nonsectarian agencies receive less religious charitable support now than in the past as the majority of giving in the black community still goes to churches and other houses of worship, which perform fewer of these functions than previously.

In addition, historically black denominations supported mission giving for religious work in foreign countries. Although formal missions agencies in black denominations did not begin until the last decade of the nineteenth century, individual missionaries such as Lott Carey and others received some support from black congregations. When black churches and denominations began their formal foreign missions agencies, these organizations drew on both support from individuals in congregations and the giving, both voluntary and apportioned, of the congregations themselves.[7] They supported not only evangelism, but educational and economic efforts consistent with the holistic vision they brought to their own American situation. This commitment to foreign missions reflected a clear, though not universal, sense of a connection to Africa as part of African American sensibilities. black denominations in the late eighteenth and early nineteenth centuries proudly claimed the title "African" and other derivatives in their names, such as the African Methodist Episcopal Church and the African Methodist Episcopal Zion Church. Congregations did the same as in the common First African Baptist Church, Abyssinian Baptist Church, or the African Church of St. Thomas, or even the use of African saints as patrons as in St. Augustine's Presbyterian or St. Cyprian's Roman Catholic Church. Foreign missions in these congregations built upon biblical texts such as Psalm 68:31, "Princes shall come forth from Egypt and Ethiopia shall stretch forth her hand unto God." Connecting with and supporting uplift in Africa was a signal part of congregational and denominational giving in the nineteenth century. It is no accident that African missions increased exponentially in the latter part of that century during the rise of Pan Africanism. The point for our discussion is to see how financial support for religious institutions channeled its way beyond the immediate goals of local congregational maintenance. To the extent that African American religious giving no longer reflects such efforts—especially the connection to Africa—would indicate a retreat from prophetic philanthropy.[8]

Religious Charities and African American Religion

This does not mean that houses of worship served as the only service organizations in premodern black America. Other institutions, such as schools, mutual aid societies, nursing homes, and even libraries served distinct communities when support was available.

In the early days of the United States, houses of worship not only educated their own members within the congregation, they supported the educational efforts of other institutions, almost invariably religious in nature. In addition to the southern schools attended by persons such as Mays and Kelsey, black schools and colleges grew through the combined efforts of black and white philanthropy, much of it religious in nature. In the case of those schools that grew to become what we now call "historically black colleges and universities," individual charity joined with apportioned giving by black congregations and denominations to support educational efforts. The African Methodist Episcopal Church, the largest of the historically black Methodist denominations, began efforts to have schools sponsored in every jurisdiction of their work, beginning in 1844. In 1863, they took control of a small struggling Methodist school in Tawawa Springs, Ohio, and developed both Wilberforce University and Payne Theological Seminary from its foundation. Black Baptists began schools such as Morehouse College, Virginia Union University, and Shaw University with the assistance of some white denominational and philanthropic support. The African Methodist Episcopal Zion denomination began Livingstone College, while the Colored (now Christian) Methodist Episcopal Church founded colleges such as Miles and Lane.[9]

In all cases, the support of religious institutions represented a significant share of the income for these schools. Indeed, many of them began primarily for the training of ministers and educators—preachers and teachers—whose professional goals were to advance the race in the wake of recent emancipation. Their curricula reflected a distinct religious orientation and community service agenda. Charitable giving to these schools was an investment in the uplift of the black community, not simply support of education for education's sake, or even the type of bald preprofessionalism that characterizes too much of contemporary college curricula.

Even predominantly white denominations began or adopted black schools, and merged their resources with those of African American individuals and religious institutions. The Episcopal Church joined in with the heroic fundraising efforts of Tuskegee graduate Elizabeth Evelyn Wright to strengthen Voorhees College; Presbyterians developed Biddle Institute (now Johnson C. Smith University) and Lincoln University; the Disciples of Christ supported the development of Jarvis Christian College; while the Methodist (now United Methodist) Church joined with Mary McLeod Bethune in the development of Bethune Cookman College. The Methodists also sponsored a number of colleges that eventually became public institutions, such as Morgan State University and the University of Maryland, Eastern Shore.

The drama in mentioning these institutions lies in the support drawn from the congregations and denominations that sponsored them. Sometimes there were specific offerings taken for the schools, other times there was direct denominational support through the budgeting and apportionment process. And this does not include the countless number of times congregations would simply take an offering for the direct support of one of their own young people in order for them to attend college. Former Philadelphia mayor Wilson Goode often speaks of having attended a high school where the guidance counselor told him he was not college material. While working in a neighborhood factory, his pastor pulled him aside and told him that he needed to be in college. His church, First Baptist Church of Paschall, raised the money to send him to Morgan State in Baltimore, a journey that led him through graduate school, public service, and ordained ministry to his current work leading a national movement for the mentoring of children of prisoners.[10] Many congregations still provide some scholarship support. Sadly, the amounts given have not kept pace with rising costs of education, and the money that once supported a student for a year or more now barely buys books for one class.

The Mutual Aid societies of the late eighteenth and early nineteenth centuries served African Americans in areas of health care, insurance, and economic development. Individual and congregational support of these institutions played a vital role in keeping their doors open for those seeking relief from financial distress, help with basic medical services, insurance in the cases of illness, or death and basic community services and advocacy. The latter roles, served by the institutions of the social justice and civil rights industry in the twentieth century, reflected the prophetic tradition of African American Christianity. Their ability to speak out against racism and racist practices, such as slavery, segregation, and discrimination, depended upon a strong, independent financial base. Houses of worship participated in such support, both in service delivery and advocacy. To the extent that contemporary congregations still provide social services but without the attending social advocacy, they stray from the prophetic tradition, and financial support of their work falls short of African American prophetic philanthropy.

Social gospel agencies such as the Colored YMCA movement both drew on donations from black religious institutions and the leadership within those institutions. Benjamin Mays worked for the Colored YMCAs in the 1920s and 1930s. Mordecai Johnson, the first African American president of Howard University, cut his teeth as a fundraiser with the Colored YMCAs. The Colored YMCAs of this era clearly identified themselves as religious organizations, even to the point where some churches felt threatened by them (which also hindered fundraising efforts from African American congregations). Their mission included the social betterment and uplift aims of the social gospel era, and black churches supplied them with leadership and some income. Again, to the extent that black congregational dollars went into these efforts, African American religious institutions supported social betterment efforts outside of their congregations, but almost always within the framework of their own commitment to community advancement.[11]

Other institutions, such as nursing homes and libraries, shared this legacy. In nineteenth-century Philadelphia, the Stephen Smith Home for the Aged (founded through the will of an African American businessman and A.M.E. preacher who died in 1873) saw such support as did the Colored Library of Philadelphia. In the twentieth century, Pentecostal denominations developed social institutions that relied heavily upon donations and other support from congregations. The Mount Sinai Holy Church of America, the first black denomination to be headed by a woman, Bishop Ida Robinson, began a nursing home in Philadelphia in the 1950s. The New York City–based Mount Calvary Holy Church began a job training and placement center in the 1930s. Both denominations also owned for-profit farming operations that assisted in fund development, as well as employment opportunities for the poor during this period.

Finally, in an initiative prefiguring the development of church-based community development corporations in the latter quarter of the twentieth century, larger, urban African American churches developed social welfare centers in the early decades of the 1900s to meet various social and community needs. Relying heavily on investments from both the host and other congregations, these centers provided everything from food and clothing distribution to job training and placement. Several bore the title of "Institutional" churches, signifying their identification with the social gospel movement and its attempt to form Christian churches into multipurpose social welfare organizations providing comprehensive services in poor neighborhoods. These congregations, such as Williams Institutional Colored Methodist Episcopal Church in Harlem, and Institutional African Methodist Episcopal Church in Chicago, were led by educated clergy who believed in a comprehensive approach to community-based ministry. The Chicago Church was led by Reverdy Cassius Ransome, who later became a bishop in the AME Church, and attracted such members as Ida Wells to its ministry of social service and advocacy. Williams Institutional, led by Yale Ph.D. William Bell, was noted for its work in economic development, and support of the Universal Negro Improvement Association and the philosophy of Marcus Garvey.[12] African American financial support of these congregations and their outreach centers reflected a philanthropic press toward not only community betterment in the name of religion, but also a nascent form of Pan-African and Black Nationalistic thought as a ground for advocacy work in the black community. This development provides an interesting transition to African American religion, philanthropy and social advocacy.

Houses of Worship and Support
for Social Causes

African American religious historian Gayraud Wilmore points
to the era between the Reconstruction period and World War
I as one characterized by "the Deradicalization of the Black
Church" and "the Dechristianization of Black Radicalism."[13]
By this, Wilmore refers to both a decline in social advocacy
within black churches themselves, and a growing number of
secular organizations who took up the mantle of social protest.
In the case of the former, Wilmore points to the growing social conservatism of African American churches directly related
to increased emphasis on individualized charity, and the rise of
Booker T. Washington as chief spokesman for black American
aspirations. Wilmore contextualizes these developments within
the framework of increased and even violent opposition to and
repression of black efforts in the post-Reconstruction era, and
the need to deal with the abject poverty created in both rural Southern and urban Northern communities. In either case,
space was created for social advocacy to arise from nonsectarian
sources, such as the National Association for the Advancement
of Colored People and the National Urban League.

While the Urban League clearly depended on the private
sector for much of its support, it was not without investments
and contributions from religious organizations. The NAACP
depended more heavily on philanthropic giving, as well as membership, the latter often promoted by the religious community.
In many communities, the leadership of both the religious community and the local NAACP was one and the same, challenging
the notion of a deradicalized black church, and replacing it with
the more nuanced view that churches often supplied the spiritual
and moral vision for persons to exercise social advocacy work

through secular organizations. In addition, one can trace the direct support of religious congregations and organizations to the growth of the NAACP at both the local and national level.[14]

In the Civil Rights era, African American congregational support for social advocacy peaked in support of such local efforts as the Montgomery Improvement Association and the Alabama Christian Movement for Human Rights, as well as national organizations like the Southern Christian Leadership Conference. Aldon Morris and others have demonstrated the critical role the churches played in the development and support of these organizations.[15] This includes financial and other in-kind support that reflected institutional giving patterns promoting social advocacy. In the past 25 years, such advocacy has shifted to the community organization movement, with national groups such as Industrial Areas Foundation (IAF), Regional Council of Neighborhood Organizations (RCNO), Gamaliel, Direct Action and Research Training (DART) and PICO (formerly the Pacific Institute for Community Organizing) mobilizing community members and their moneys in efforts of social change.[16]

The point of the above is twofold. First, it demonstrates that channels other than individual charitable giving must be traced to see the full orbit of black giving patterns. African Americans have historically given the overwhelming majority of their individual philanthropy to their congregations. Second, those congregations then made major financial contributions to educational and social service agencies through voluntary donations and denominational apportionment. To have an accurate appraisal of black religious giving patterns, one must look at this more complex cash flow and its attendant governance structures. Similarly, individual support for or protest against such efforts can be seen by the extent to which church members vote for or against their continuance by altering giving patterns to the local church or by leaving those churches with such a philanthropic bent for congregations that spend their money in other ways.

African American Religious Institutions as Objects of General Philanthropy

Once one considers the religious nature of most African American institutions in the nineteenth and early twentieth century, the history of philanthropic giving to African American religion takes on a broader perspective. In short, to the extent that giving by such philanthropic families and institutions as Rockefeller, Carnegie, and others supported social welfare within the black community through such entities as historically black colleges and universities, they supported the religious aims of the black community itself. Such giving was not always religiously motivated; some charitable work with black institutions reflected regular giving patterns for social betterment. But religious interest motivated much of the philanthropic investment in black institutions.

At the congregational level, this is more difficult to establish, save through the stories of individual congregations that trace their histories to the largesse, sometimes altruistic and sometimes self-serving, of white wealth providing the support necessary to begin and sustain black churches, especially in the suburbs of the Northeast. In many of these communities, the need for live-in domestic servants spilled over into a need for congregations that would provide for their religious needs. A not unusual blend of black self-determination and white resistance to integration often resulted in wealthy white families providing the necessary financial support for the establishment of congregations that would become part of black denominations.

Many of these congregations were established as members of the historically black Methodist denominations, notably the African Methodist Episcopal and African Methodist Episcopal Zion traditions. This reflected the donors' desire to place these congregations within connectional church systems where there would be external oversight, a feature of Methodist church organization.

In many northern New Jersey suburban communities, these congregations have outlasted the live-in domestic era and still stand today. Interestingly, unless a black neighborhood grew up surrounding the church building these congregations subsequently became commuter churches peopled primarily by the descendants of original families from the domestic era. In many churches, the fundraising expectations of the congregation still reflect the white support of suburbanites with loyalty to the families of their domestics. Some, because they have never transitioned from such support, find contemporary fundraising more difficult without ties to white families and their institutions that was characteristic when their parents and grandparents served those families as butlers, maids, chauffeurs, gardeners, and the like. For every modern suburban megachurch serving the black middle class, there are scores of smaller black denominational congregations struggling with the realities of financial support in the current era. Contemporary giving to such congregations must increase to keep them strong and relevant to local suburban communities. Their megachurch neighbors have a more regional focus that may overlook real changes needed in their immediate vicinity.

In the 1990s the larger world of philanthropy "discovered" African American religious institutions, especially houses of worship, and the social capital they controlled. Whereas foundations such as the Pew Charitable Trusts and the Lilly

Endowments had been generous with what were now being called "faith-based institutions," other national foundations such as Ford, Annie E. Casey, and even Rockefeller found themselves moving beyond charitable giving to African American nonsectarian institutions that were committed to social welfare and uplift, and began to consider the actual power of faith as a motivating factor in the lives of religious folks and institutions as they engaged social issues.

The interest of these foundations stimulated or matched activity by local and regional foundations to support faith-based institutions in general, and African American religious institutions in particular. In some cases this meant beginning efforts to engage those communities, while in others, pre-existing efforts were expanded by the new national visibility of faith-based solutions to community problems. United Way agencies in cities such as Boston and Philadelphia invested in faith-based programs aimed toward reducing juvenile violence and crime.[17] Community foundations in cities such as Detroit, Cleveland, and Pittsburgh made similar investments and convened meetings of other local foundations to determine proper strategies of investment in religious institutions that could be implemented in keeping with these foundations' historically nonsectarian missions. At the same time, many foundations used their nonsectarian missions to mask a decidedly antireligious bias and remain distant from, or even hostile toward any partnerships with religious institutions.

During this time, African American churches, which already had a demonstrated capacity to partner with secular agencies through the development of affiliate nonprofit organizations (most often called community development corporations, whether they met the technical definition of such or no) benefited most often from this new interest. The existence of such an affiliate normally signaled the presence of an infrastructure designed to both cooperate with nonreligious agencies—public and private—through managing grant moneys and implementing programs that relegated religious doctrine to the side in favor of religiously motivated social welfare and advocacy. Historic national agencies such as the Salvation Army, Episcopal Community Services, and Catholic Charities had vast experience in this work. Larger African American religious institutions learned quickly to take advantage of this expanded seat at the table. Smaller organizations and churches found it much more difficult to become part of the mix.[18]

In virtually all cases, advocates took care to distinguish between the funding of religion itself and the support of social betterment efforts by religious individuals and institutions. The introduction of Charitable Choice to the Welfare Reform Act of 1995 made provision for faith-based institutions to compete for public dollars in certain social welfare activities and contained guidelines to effectively channel moneys to services without providing direct support to religious activities. While the implementation of such an initiative proved quite uneven from state to state, the spirit of the legislation provided some space for private philanthropy to begin to engage the faith community in ways that both fit the foundation's mission, but did not directly support such religious activities as Bible Study, worship services, and evangelism.[19]

Such a genuine interest on the part of some coincided with a different press on the part of others. Many political conservatives viewed investment in "faith-based initiatives" as a means to dismantling what they called "entitlement programs funded by public dollars." Compassionate conservatism was a strange brew, reflecting a mixture of genuine interest in assisting religious institutions to build their capacity for social services and a punitive spirit that blamed the objects of such efforts for their own malaise, and recoiling at the notion of government programs for their support.[20]

Another tension that arose in this era saw religious institutions torn between attempting to configure their mission and infrastructure for missions to take advantage of seemingly new dollars available for them from public and private agencies, and keeping a clear sense of their religious heritage and mission. In some cases, religious organizations attempted to chase dollars by developing hastily conceived responses to requests for proposals, often resulting in poor implementation—if funding was achieved at all. In others, foundations and public agencies pressed the faith community to restructure their institutions in order to be in compliance with RFP goals, sending those churches and religious institutions into a flurry of activity that redirected energy from existing missions and drained attention from the basic efforts that ensured their ongoing work as religious institutions.

At the same time, groups like the Annie E. Casey Foundations determined to find what they called a "resonance" between the foundation's mission and the work of local institutions, including houses of worship. The idea of resonance required that foundation personnel become familiar with the actual work of religious institutions themselves, and determine where the activity of these institutions mirrored the goals of family strengthening and economic success central to Casey's work in distressed communities. Because those communities often contained large numbers of African American and/or Latino residents, this required developing specific knowledge of the congregations and religious agencies in these neighborhoods. The foundation developed a specific portfolio, Faith and Families, to develop this work and assist them in knowledge development, implementation, and impact assessment of initiatives that required the identification of resonance between foundation and religious goals, and providing leadership for other philanthropic institutions as well in modeling how such partnerships could thrive.[21]

By focusing on resonance, Casey was able to move beyond (though not exclude) the larger congregations with existing capacities, and include smaller houses of worship who provided important services, but flew below the radar screen in popular community scans of available services. Many of these smaller institutions provided a quality of service clearly reflecting the social capital normally associated with religious institutions. Rather than concentrating on the efficiency of serving the largest client base possible, they focused on the quality of service and the building of relationships critical to building a neighborhood's infrastructure.[22] Because of their lack of a traditional social services infrastructure, many philanthropic institutions found it difficult to develop collaborations with these smaller religious institutions. However, relevant research revealed that through the development of intermediary organizations for these smaller institutions, capacity for collaboration increased. The intermediary organizations focused on the proper infrastructural needs for collaboration (fiscal management, grant reporting, government and/or foundation relations, and so on) while the smaller faith-based organizations were free to concentrate on the delivery of services that attracted the attention of funders in the first place.[23]

Yet these efforts remain controversial for a number of reasons. First, there still exists no real consensus concerning the proper role of religious institutions in the larger partnership between various organizations committed to social change, whether through advocacy or services. This not only reflects emerging variants in the results of research projects, but also pre-existing ambivalence in American culture about religion itself. American religious illiteracy breeds not only an ignorance of the reality of religious presence itself, but also blinds a public already skeptical about religious belief to the benefits of religious institutions in distressed communities. Second, this skepticism can degenerate into genuine hostility toward religion, especially the ways in which certain religious groups claim a monopoly on religious perspectives on social issues. While Stephen Carter, in his book *The Culture of Disbelief,* called for greater involvement of faith communities in public life, his corrective tome, *God's Name in Vain: The Rights and Wrongs of Religion in Politics*, protested that this involvement should not take the form of sectarian devotion to partisan politics. Carter pressed for a more prophetic approach to public engagement that protected the transcendent dimension of religious engagement, keeping it free to call society and culture to account, while still invested in service provision and community partnerships.[24] Third, such interest continues to deflect attention from the fundamental responsibility that African Americans have for supporting their own religious institutions and the work they do toward social change.

A Future for Religion and Philanthropy among African Americans

The increased diversity of African American religious traditions presents a challenge for the future of philanthropy and charitable giving in the black religious community. For example, the black religious community is no longer uniformly Christian. It remains for others to provide strong data and prospects for philanthropy among African American Muslims, Bahia, Buddhists, and other faiths. Also, as blacks migrate to the United States from Africa and the Caribbean, they tend to form congregations reflecting their immediate national and/or cultural heritage, making their giving patterns more reflective of the black churches of the eighteenth and nineteenth centuries which were clearly focused on care within the immediate community.

However, an additional consideration looms large for our discussion, namely the nondenominational churches, which are growing in many areas more rapidly than their traditional denominational counterparts. Two developments within this movement speak directly to charitable giving.

First, these congregations tend to function without a strong centralized denominational infrastructure, making the efforts black denominations launched in pooling resources to support the growth of college, schools and sustained missionary activity next to impossible. Save for some megacongregations, which undertake such work from their own resources, there is no real infrastructure that could support the creation of black colleges, hospitals, senior citizens centers, and other social service institutions except through partnerships and contracting with government agencies that can supply additional capacity.

The larger congregations may be involved in educational efforts, but these are often either private or alternative schools, which do serve to support a larger social mission in light of failing educational systems in many black communities. To the extent that congregations support these efforts, they continue the tradition of religious giving in support of service delivery characteristic of earlier eras. However, most of these schools top off before the high school years, leaving their constituencies with few alternatives to public education when young people reach adolescence. This is clearly an area where philanthropic investment should turn if the continuum of religious-based alternative education is to be constructed in a manner that more fully serves the community.

Other educational efforts organized by these congregations are mainly Bible and ministerial training programs, which provide courses in the religious tradition itself, as well as leadership and life skills for congregants and other constituencies. In these institutions, congregational giving and underwriting are often not necessary, as the schools derive income from tuition and fees collected. The infrastructure does not require extensive funding, because these schools do not seek accreditation, nor do they serve to prepare persons for work in the professional fields. Hence, these institutions and institutes do not reflect earlier religious efforts to train a cadre of religious, educational, and social service professionals who will by virtue of their vocation; contribute to the social uplift of their communities. Individuals and families may be helped by certain therapeutically designed courses to help with personal and relational challenges, but no generation of religiously trained professionals will emerge from these schools in their present state. To the extent that charitable giving supports these institutions, it is discontinuous with historic norms of social support and uplift.

Secondly, the impact of integration and its attendant shift in African American demographics has led to a geographic distancing from the poor and an attendant decline in charitable efforts toward them. Historic black church-based financial assistance and giving supported persons in need in the community—who were often members of the congregation as well. As African American houses of worship have grown and prospered, their members relocate to more affluent neighborhoods, thereby creating both a physical and cognitive distance between themselves and the people left behind in the old neighborhood.[25] Like Nehemiah, they must be reminded that the conditions among those left behind are dire: "the walls are down and the gates burned with fire" (see Nehemiah 2:13).

The connection between those neighborhoods and the black middle-class families and individuals who moved away, wanes with passing generations. Baby boomers that were born near these older congregations have some emotional ties because of their childhood proximity. Their children, many now young adults themselves, do not. As these younger adults take leadership in congregations, the press for a ministry connection to social causes in poor neighborhoods becomes less self-evident.

Third, many African American congregations, and even some denominationally-based counterparts, have adopted a message of prosperity in which the focus on giving degenerates to an investment strategy that primarily benefits the giver. This differs from the prosperity gospel of late nineteenth and early twentieth-century Christianity. When the gospel of wealth doctrines emerged under the influence of such men as Russell Conwell, and Andrew Carnegie, their speaking, preaching and writing tied the accumulation of wealth to the responsibility to use this gain for charitable purposes.[26] The Carnegie name dots the buildings of many historically black colleges and universities, including Tuskegee, Central State (a division of the African Methodist Episcopal Church's Wilberforce College when constructed), and Howard, as a testament to Carnegie's application of his responsible wealth and philanthropy gospel. Russell Conwell and his church, The Baptist Temple of Philadelphia, began a small college for the working classes of that city who could not afford more prestigious and expensive schools such as the University of Pennsylvania. Many African Americans have benefited from Conwell's application of the principles of wealth accumulation and redistribution through their attendance at Temple University.

Contemporary prosperity preaching has been notably void of such a redirection of accumulated wealth. Rather, it has tended toward pressing the accumulation of wealth with the favor of God, without an attending responsibility for generous giving and philanthropic altruism. Some megachurches have begun to respond to this lacuna through new investments in community development. But even in these cases, their work flies well under the radar screen, beneath the loud sounding blips of accumulation.

At the same time, other congregations, such as Concord Baptist Church of Christ in Brooklyn, New York, have begun their own foundations, reasoning that their ability to attract and accumulate resources places them in a position to both leverage moneys from larger foundations and to challenge their members to be more proactive in their personal philanthropy.

The problem rests not so much in a new-found materialism in the black community as it does in a critical acceptance of the postmodern worldview that reads life through the lens of personal fulfillment, efficacy, efficiency, and therapy.[27] In short, religious institutions have lost their "countercultural" perspective on the world and its ideas, and seems now to be hell-bent (pun intended) on helping individuals find their place in that world. Altruism, sacrifice, and relationship-building find themselves replaced by a theology of giving that primarily benefits the giver. Leaders present religious giving in terms of investments, "seed-faith," and "sowing for a return." One can almost hear the text from the Gospel of Luke changed from "Give *and* it shall be given unto you. . . ." to "Give *so* it will be given unto you."

The remedy for such self-referential charity resides in a renewed call to altruism within religious congregations. This squares with a recapturing of the etymological root of the term philanthropy—love of humanity. The uncritical acceptance of a worldview that places blame for each individual's malaise on his own decision making, paired with a command to pick oneself up by the bootstraps, renders altruism weak in the contemporary religious mind. Simply put, unless religious congregations return to the prophetic roots of their tradition, and challenge the self-centered, consumerist ethos of the present age, philanthropy will never return to the prophetic character it once represented.

This is not to say that the tradition has died. Indeed, prophetic voices continue to cry aloud amidst the competing voices of the culture. The recently formed Samuel DeWitt Proctor Conference, consisting on a number of African American congregations from across the country, has given considerable attention to the need for a new altruism, focusing signal attention to community-rebuilding efforts in New Orleans, and linking their larger congregations with smaller struggling churches in their communities in order to spread the wealth of empowerment.[28] The community-organizing efforts detailed earlier in this essay testify to ongoing support for this same prophetic tradition.

This is not to say that nonprophetic activity has no place. Even the most politically conservative or even apolitical congregation provides basic social and family services that would cost hundreds of thousands of dollars to replace in most communities if left to nonsectarian agencies.[29] When congregations and their members visit the sick and give food and clothing to the needy, when pastors provide marital and grief counseling, when choirs and Sunday Schools provide religious activities for youth, there is merit and value that would be seriously missed if all houses of worship closed their doors. Yet, the fact remains that without concerted pressure toward social change and advocacy, congregations who receive their income from the donations of individuals can offer only a truncated mission in comparison with that of their predecessors. For religious philanthropy to be maximized in the black community, the religious vision for social uplift and change must be rekindled, and the holistic efforts for community change recaptured: No matter how much money passes through our religious institutions, it matters to what cause it flows.

Recommendations

In light of the traditions and changes within the giving patterns of African Americans and their religious institutions, one can posit the following challenges and recommendations for present and future work:

- African Americans must resist the growing trend for their giving to houses of worship to be spent increasingly on institutional maintenance. The more that percentage grows, the less money flows outside the congregation to other noteworthy causes and institutions outside of the congregation. Only a few congregations will be able to counter that they have the capacity to maintain the diversity of services (education, health care, employment) that characterized their eighteenth- and nineteenth-century ancestors. As such, there is less African American money available for these services, which were once housed within the church.
- African American religious leaders must revisit their philosophy and theology of giving, wresting it from the self-interested notions of the contemporary prosperity movement and cultivating a sense and spirit of altruism, generosity, and philanthropy. Prosperity is not the enemy; prosperity for prosperity's sake is the culprit.
- Parallel to such a shift is the development of a critique of consumerism. This goes beyond notions of conspicuous consumption to the heart of the consumerist ethic, namely that people, even religious people, choose to spend their money on whatever they want. The religious alternative posits an ethic of stewardship, which argues that all money and

possessions belong to the Creator and the believer places her or his goods and wealth at God's disposal.

- African American congregations must exert leadership, both locally and denominationally, to oversee the dollars that pass through congregations to larger efforts such as missions, education, social agencies and the like. To the extent that these dollars are diverted to institutional maintenance (that is, keeping the denomination going or its leadership prosperous), they minimize potential support for historic institutions such as the HBCU (Historically Black Colleges and Universities)—especially those still maintaining connection to church bodies, health care and social welfare, and advocacy institutions such as the NAACP, the Urban League, the YMCA, and others.

- The struggles and even closings of HBCUs begun and operated by historically black churches offends the memory of those congregations and denominations which birthed and nurtured them through their infancy. While many lament the disproportionate numbers of young black males in prison versus those in college, few lament the hardships (such as Morris Brown and Knoxville Colleges) and demise (such as Kittrell and Bishop Colleges) of the colleges to which they would have had access. Religious giving to colleges at the denominational, congregational, and individual level must increase if the black community is serious about educational opportunities for the marginalized of our community.

- African Americans must financially support small to midsize congregations that provide the type of social capital and networks that strengthen neighborhoods and communities. The megachurch phenomenon can divert attention from the realities of relationship building that characterized the strong neighborhood support systems of earlier generations.

- The philanthropic community must grow in its recognition of the social value of religious institutions, and develop even more ways of supporting this work. When the foundation community claims either ignorance of religious institutions, or reluctance to support sectarian approaches to social welfare, it must be confronted with the following: In many of the most distressed communities in our country, the most visible, legally sanctioned institutions in those neighborhoods are houses of worship and bars. Given the choice of where to put their money in developing networks of social support for those neighborhoods, which will they choose?

- Also, there exist two competing philosophies of giving that clash both within religious institutions, and in the tensions between the larger philanthropic world and religion itself. Simply put, this is the tension between quantity and quality of services. Quantity of service often comes masked in the otherwise innocuous notion of "measurable outcomes." Borrowed from the for-profit world, this more bang for the buck reflects the press of foundations seeking to please boards of directors accustomed to measuring success by the bottom line. Many religious institutions do not operate that way. Without making excuses for waste or duplicity in their management of resources, many religious institutions reflect flexibility in programming that enables them to focus on the quality of outreach, and not a simple McService ethic that equates success with numbers served. Foundations must find more ways to support such quality of service efforts. Religious institutions must resist attempts to sacrifice quality for quantity in the attempt to chase external support for their efforts.

- Returning to religious institutions for a word of summation, we press religious institutions to recapture their prophetic voice as champions of those oppressed, distressed, and marginalized by social, cultural, and racial arrangements. While some would argue that recent efforts to provide government support for religious social services has muted the prophetic voice of black religion, others point to a waning prophetic voice in the years prior to the promotion of faith-based initiatives. Gayraud Wilmore's pointing to the late-nineteenth- and early-twentieth-century "Dechristianization of Black Radicalism" and the "Deradicalization of the Black Church," the rise and subsequent decline of religious support for civil rights issues, and the entrenchment of the modern self-interested prosperity movement, even before, government interest in supporting faith-based institutions—all these point beyond external forces culpable of the weakening of the prophetic. Ultimately, African Americans and their houses of worship must determine whether the prophetic voice is inherent to their religious traditions, or if it only flourishes when their own interests are the beneficiaries of prophetic witness. If to be religious one must be prophetic—then religious giving will reflect such a champion's spirit. If not, expect to see more and more of religious giving remain within the walls (figuratively and literally) of our houses of worship.

Notes

1. Dean Hoge, Charles Zech, Michael Donahue, and Patrick McNamara, *Money Matters: Personal Giving in American Churches* (Louisville, KY: Westminster/John Knox, 1996), p. 13.
2. Russell N. James III and Deanna Sharpe, "The 'Sect Effect' in Charitable Giving: Distinctive Realities of Exclusively Religious Charitable Givers," *The American Journal of Economics and Sociology* (October 1, 2007).

3. See the website of the National Black United Fund, www.nbuf.org/ statistics. See also, Julia McCord, "Contributions to Churches Vary," *Omaha (Neb.) World-Herald*, April 23, 2000; and James Prichard, "Philanthropy Growing among People of Color," *Detroit News*, January 13, 2001.

4. A number of texts have appeared over time supporting this notion. Among the best are C. Eric Lincoln and Lawrence Mamiya's *The Black Church in the African American Experience* (Durham, NC: Duke University Press, 1990); and Andrew Billingsley's *Mighty Like A River: The Black Church and Social Reform* (New York: Oxford University Press, 2003). Tysus Jackson, building on the work of E. Franklin Frazier, Emmett Carson, and others, shows the connection to historic giving patterns in his article "Young African Americans: A New Generation of Giving Behaviour," *International Journal of Nonprofit and Voluntary Sector Marketing*. 6, no. 3 (2001). Jackson's article is instructive because of his examination of various motivations, including religious, for giving. As we will see, even within the African American religious tradition, motivations for giving are varied.

5. Harold Dean Trulear, "George Kelsey, Christianity and Race: A View from the Academy," *Princeton Theological Review* 10:2 (2004): 35–36; Mays rehearses his journey in his *Born to Rebel: An Autobiography* (Athens, GA: University of Georgia, 2003).

6. See especially Cheryl Townsend Gilkes, "The Black Church as a Therapeutic Community: Areas of Suggested Research into the Black Religious Experience," *Journal of the Interdenominational Theological Center* 8, no. 1 (1980): 29–44.

7. Leroy Fitts has chronicled both the life of black Baptist missionary Lott Carey and the convention that bears his name in *Lott Carey: First Black Missionary to Africa* (Valley Forge, PA: Judson, 1978); and *The Lott Carey Legacy of African American Missions* (Baltimore: Gateway Press, 1994).

8. George Washington Williams chronicles much of this as a virtual eyewitness and historian in his centennial publication *A History of the Negro Race in America, 1619–1880* (New York: G.P. Putnam's Sons, 1883). Gayraud Wilmore makes a clear case for this connection, as well as the connection between foreign missions and Pan Africanism rehearsed below in his standard text *Black Religion and Black Radicalism:*

An Interpretation of the Religious History of African Americans (Maryknoll, NY: Orbis, 2003), pp.125–162.

9. See Paul Griffin's *Black Theology in the Foundation of Three Methodist Colleges: The Educational Views and Labors of Daniel Payne, Joseph Price and Isaac Lane* (Lanham, MD: University Press of America, 1984), for an exemplary account of this relationship. The popular text, *I'll Find a Way or Make One: A Tribute to Historically Black Colleges and Universities* (New York: Amistad/Harper Collins, 2004) by Juan Williams and Duane Ashley contains a number of accounts of the founding of these and other schools.

10. Course Lecture by Wilson Goode in his class "Community Renewal," taught at Eastern Baptist Theological Seminary, Summer Session 2000.

11. Nina Mjagkaj chronicles this tension between black churches and the YMCA movement in *Light in the Darkness: African Americans and the YMCA, 1852–1946* (Lexington: University of Kentucky, 1994), especially pp. 39–44, where the tension is clearly traced. For an example of a positive relationship between black churches and the YMCA's see Harold Dean Trulear, "There's A Bright Side Somewhere: Some Preliminary Observations on the Role of the Church in Black Migration," *Journal of the Afro-American Historical and Genealogical Society* 8 (1987): 2.

12. See Randall Burkett's treatment of Bell in *Garveyism as a Religious Movement: the Institutionalization of a Black Civil Religion* (Metuchen, NJ: Scarecrow Press, 1978), pp. 168–171.

13. See Wilmore's *Black Religion and Black Radicalism,* pp. 163–221.

14. Trulear, "There's A Bright Side."

15. See Aldon Morris, *The Origins of the Civil Rights Movement: Black Communities Organizing for Change* (New York: Free Press, 1986).

16. Examples are cited in Dennis Jacobsen's *Doing Justice: Congregations and Community Organizing* (Minneapolis: Augsburg, 2001); and Richard Woods' *Faith in Action: Religion, Race, and Democratic Organizing in America* (Chicago: University of Chicago, 2002), both of which document the work of community organizing strategies among African American congregations.

17. The United Way of Massachusetts Bay created a Faith in Action network consisting of religious institutions, community organizations, and local philanthropies that sought to strengthen communities through community-based partnerships and giving. Their efforts included the publication of a guide for assessing the effectiveness of faith based organizations in social service delivery entitled *Inside Out: Tools to Help Faith Based Organizations Measure, Learn and Grow* (Baltimore, MD: The Annie E. Casey Foundation, 2000).

18. See John DiIulio, "Supporting Black Churches" *Brookings Review* 17 (Spring 1999).

19. Amy Sherman, "The Growing Impact of Charitable Choice," *Center for Public Justice* (2000); David Bositis, "The Black Church and the Faith Based Initiative," *Joint Center for Political and Economic Studies* (2006).

20. I treat this development more substantively in "Faith and the Public Square," *Visions and Values* 12, no. 2 (2004).

21. Paula Dressel, *Faith and Families: A Decade Review, 1998–2007* (Baltimore, MD: The Annie E. Casey Foundation, 2008).

22. See examples in Cynthia Milsap and Bernice Taylor, *The Black Churches of West Humboldt Park* (Chicago: Egan Urban Center at DePaul University, 1999).

23. See Amy Sherman, "Faith in Communities: A Solid Investment," *Society* (Jan/Feb 2003): 19–26; and Harold Dean Trulear, "Offering Intermediaries," *The Challenge of Faith* 1, no. 2 (2002).

24. *The Culture of Disbelief* (New York: Anchor, 1994) was subtitled "How American Law and Politics Trivialize Religious Devotion." *God's Name in Vain* (New York: Basic Books, 2001) takes its title from the C.S. Lewis essay "Meditations on the Third Commandment" found in his collection *God in the Dock* (Grand Rapids, MI: Wm. B. Eerdmans, 1994) originally published in 1941 giving caution against the idea of a "Christian political party."

25. An excellent case study demonstrating the problems in such a congregation is found in Ida Mukenge's *The Black Church in Urban America: A Case Study in Political Economy*, (Lanham, MD: University Press of America, 1983). I also examine this phenomenon in more detail in my essay "The Black Middle Class Church and the Quest for Community," *The Drew Gateway*, 42. no. 1 (1992).

26. See the collection *The Autobiography of Andrew Carnegie and the Gospel of Wealth* (New York: Signet, 2006); Conwell's essay *Acres of Diamonds* has been reprinted in a number of sources, including a recent reprint from Wilder Publications in 2008.

27. I am indebted to the sociological writings of Shane Lee and Milmon Harrison for their insights to what I would term the postmodern captivity of African American Christianity. Both Lee's scholarly biography *T.D. Jakes: America's New Preacher* (New York: NYU Press, 2005), and Harrison's case study *Righteous Riches: The Word of Faith Movement in Contemporary African American Religion* (New York: Oxford University Press, 2005), clearly articulate this connection without caricature or venom. Similarly, my impulse is not to personally attack or indict specific figures or ministries, which I deem counterproductive for the age. Rather, I am calling for a renewed investment in cultural analysis for the purpose of reclaiming the prophetic tradition. The enemy is neither greed nor simple self interest—it is captivity to a narcissistic consumerist culture that, unaddressed, becomes the lens through which religious texts, experiences, and life are viewed.

28. See the volume edited by Proctor Conference members Jeremiah Wright, Frederick Haynes, and Iva Carruthers, *Blow the Trumpet in Zion: Global Vision and Action for the 21st Century Black Church* (Minneapolis: Augsburg Fortress Press, 2005), for important essays detailing the vision for this vision of empowerment.

29. Ram Cnaan has pioneered the monetary quantification of the value of church-based social service provision. See especially his *The Other Philadelphia Story: How Local Congregations Support the Quality of Life in Urban America*, written with Stephanie Boddie, Charlene McGrew, and Jennifer Kang (Philadelphia: University of Pennsylvania Press, 2006). Chapter 7, "Black Congregations in the City of Brotherly Love" deals specifically with African American congregations.

Chapter 3

Fundraising to Strengthen Black Communities

Birgit Smith Burton
Senior Director for Foundation Relations,
Georgia Institute of Technology, Atlanta, GA

The Facts

U.S. Charitable Giving

- Giving USA Foundation, which publishes the yearbook of philanthropy researched and written by the Center on Philanthropy at Indiana University, reported that U.S. charitable giving reached an estimated $306.39 billion in 2007 exceeding $300 billion for the first time in history.[1]
- Individual donations, including bequests, accounted for more than 82 percent of the total with gifts tallying $252 billion.[2]

- Overall, giving was up 3.9 percent, with every charitable subsector receiving donations showing an increase in 2007 with religious organizations continuing to receive the biggest share of donations accounting for 33.4 percent of the total giving.[3]
- Corporations accounted for more than $15.6 billion—5.1 percent; and foundations accounted for $38.5 billion—12.6 percent, which is slightly more than a 10 percent increase over 2006.[4]
- The growth in foundation giving may be attributed to the growing pace of wealth transfer. Foundations (not including corporate foundations) have increased in number as well as giving. The growth in foundation giving increased less than 1 percent per year from 1967 to 1990 but 9.5 percent from 1991 to 2005.[5]

Nonprofit Organizations

- According to the National Center for Charitable Statistics (NCCS), the national clearinghouse of data on the nonprofit sector in the United States, there were 1.4 million nonprofit organizations registered in the United States as of January 2008.[6]
- A representative from the NCCS stated that it is impossible to single out those organizations that are run by African Americans or whose mission is to provide assistance to African Americans because there is not a place on the IRS tax form that requests that information.

Introduction

As evidenced throughout American history, nonprofit organizations have played a vital role in protecting the freedoms and democracy we treasure as a society, and play an equally important role today as our social and economic needs continue to evolve. The success and longevity of these institutions is fundamentally tied to the generosity of individual American philanthropists, who make up the greatest percentage of giving in the country. For African Americans, there exists an opportunity to uplift the health, vibrancy, and strength of our community by uniting in support of our nonprofit organizations.

Empowered by greater levels of individual wealth and education, along with diminishing levels of discrimination, African American donors are an increasingly significant segment of the individual donor population. In order to meet their goals, nonprofit organizations need to recognize the diverse needs and interests of the black philanthropist and communicate accordingly. Further, in order to earn respect and credibility from the African American donor, these nonprofits—whether focused on African American causes in the community or addressing global needs—must exhibit organizational strength in the form of healthy finances and a clearly articulated mission. These nonprofits will go further in achieving their mission by cultivating effective fundraisers who both understand the diversity of the donor population and who themselves reflect the donor populations they serve.

Nonprofit Organizations in America

American society began to take shape long before government services appeared on the scene. Early Americans had to find ways to provide public services themselves, if they were to be provided at all. They partnered with their neighbors to establish schools, construct public facilities, and build the social infrastructure needed to create a sense of community. As American society became more complex, so, too, did the need for public and social services. In response to these new and changing needs, these previously informal partnerships evolved, over the past 150 years, into ever more formalized and specialized organizations.[7]

For much of American history, however, African Americans were excluded from participation in the various groups and businesses as well as public and private entities that were being created to assist the white majority.[8] African Americans, out of sheer necessity, began developing mutual aid and benevolent societies to take care of their own social needs. They also began building their own religious, business, and educational institutions as well. One of the most successful of these efforts was the United Negro College Fund, which was founded to support the private schools that were educating blacks at a time when few states would support their education with public funds.[9]

Today, according to the National Center for Charitable Statistics (NCCS), there are nearly 1.5 million nonprofit organizations in the United States, filling many critical roles in American society. Dr. Lester M. Salamon, director of the Center for Civil Society Studies at the Johns Hopkins University, examined the role and importance of nonprofit organizations in American life and noted in his article "Nonprofit Organizations: America's Invisible Sector":

> *Few aspects of American society are more revealing of American character, or more central to American life, than the thousands of day-care centers, clinics, hospitals, higher-education institutions, civic action groups, museums, symphonies, environmental groups and related organizations that comprise America's private, nonprofit sector.*

America's nonprofit sector has traditionally functioned as "a flexible mechanism through which people concerned about a social or economic problem can begin to respond without having to convince a majority of their fellow citizens that the problem deserves a more general government response."[10] In addition, America's nonprofit sector has helped to achieve and protect our freedom and democracy. Most of the social movements over the past century—women's suffrage, the labor movement, the civil rights movement, the anti-war movement, and the environmental movement, among others—began in the nonprofit sector.[11]

Officially, a nonprofit organization is a corporation formed to carry out a charitable, educational, religious, literary, or scientific purpose. These organizations typically support themselves by raising public and private grant money as well as donations from individuals and corporations. Donations to such organizations may be tax-deductible to the donor while the nonprofit organization itself benefits from certain federal, state, income, property, and sales tax-exemptions. Federal and state governments generally do not tax nonprofit organizations on money they earn that is directly related to their nonprofit purpose because of the benefits they contribute to society. However, all funds received by the organization must be used to further its charitable mission.

African American Support for Nonprofits: Credibility is the Bottom Line

Successful nonprofit organizations play a vital role in creating and sustaining social capital, which is the foundation of a vibrant and healthy community. One way for black communities to ensure their health, strength, and vitality is to unite in support of the nonprofit organizations that serve and help sustain them. These organizations address many important issues in African

American communities, ranging from health and education disparities to social and economic mores. Over the years, they have provided a vision and impetus for change that has been fundamental to the protection of the rights and freedoms of African Americans, and they have actively fought for social justice and equality as well.

As the inequality gap closes and the issues that initially fueled the creation of many of these nonprofits continue to improve, many African Americans today question the need to continue to support these organizations. By illuminating—and thereby segregating—the needs of the black community, the work of these organizations is viewed as counterproductive to forging an equal society. More and more, African Americans have giving interests that are reflective of their own experience. Greater levels of individual wealth and a perceived decrease in racial discrimination have empowered blacks to give to nonprofits other than the church or those that exclusively have an African American focus. Fueled by their own achievements, this segment of the African American community may not necessarily want to be reminded of the hardships and adverse conditions that, while diminishing over time, still exist for large numbers of the African American population.[12]

By and large, African Americans are exhibiting greater discretion, in general, when considering support for any nonprofit organization that may offer a solution to a community, national, or global need. Emmet D. Carson[13], in a chapter of *New Directions for Philanthropic Fundraising*, notes: "For nonprofit organizations that do not have an African American focus, there exist new opportunities to recruit African American donors in support of their work." In doing so, African Americans are, in their own right, discriminating among the millions of nonprofits that rely on private philanthropy to steward their missions.[14]

So how can nonprofit organizations *in* the African American community hope to be supported *by* the African American community? The answer is inherent in the strength of the organizations themselves. The organizations that will gain the respect and, therefore, the support of the African American philanthropic community are the ones that exhibit financial solvency, consistency in their mission, excellence in programming, measurable results, and internal leadership that empowers the organization to achieve its goals. The strength of the nonprofit community is also dependent on the degree to which board and staff members of the organization hold themselves accountable for delivering on their promises. While trust is implicit in the traditional philanthropic model of giving to the Church, that same trust needs to be earned by the nonprofits that are receiving emerging support from the African American community.

Fundraising—Whose Job Is It?

The strength and credibility of a nonprofit organization heavily depends on its fundraising efforts. Organizations must be willing to invest in the people, resources, and technologies needed to ensure they can consistently and effectively deliver on the promises inherent in their missions. Those responsible for fundraising are tasked with cultivating and soliciting individual donors, as well as managing the often complex and time-consuming process of soliciting grants from foundations and corporations. Who should be responsible for raising the funds for an organization? Is it the development director, fundraising consultant, executive director, or members of the board? Often the decision of who should be responsible for fundraising is dictated by the organization's budget; yet, every organization should have at least one individual whose main responsibility is to generate philanthropic support for the organization.

The executive director has numerous responsibilities and fundraising is usually among them, even if the organization has a consultant or a professional fundraiser on staff. The executive director is basically the chief development officer because he or she is typically the recognized face of the organization, the one who signs the solicitation and acknowledgement letters, who participates in site visits with funders, and who loses the most sleep worrying about how to keep the organization's doors open and lights on.

The organization's board is always charged with the ultimate responsibility of fundraising no matter who on staff is leading the fundraising effort. The board should be 100 percent supportive of the organization's fundraising effort: first, because if they don't believe in the organization enough to support it, how can they credibly convince others to do so? Second, a growing number of institutional funders expect to see such support, regardless of the amount of their contributions. Generally speaking, board members unwilling to support their organization with their money as well as their time should not be on the board.

Investing in a fundraising program, particularly fundraising staff, can certainly lead to greater success. The Kresge Foundation demonstrated this point when it established the Kresge HBCU Initiative[15]—a five-year, $18 million program designed to build and support improved fundraising efforts at historically black colleges and universities (HBCUs). The goal was to help five of these colleges and universities develop stronger, self-sustaining advancement operations. The HBCU initiative provided each grantee with the resources to develop a comprehensive advancement program to strengthen their fundraising efforts. Dr. Norman Francis, president of Xavier University, one of the grantee institutions, said that "prior to the Kresge Initiative, we had no way to raise money." With additional support that included ensuring adequate staffing, implementing improved technologies, and defining standard policies and procedures, each of the five recipients was able to develop a continuous program of prospect cultivation.[16] Billie Sue Schulze, program director and author of *Changing the Odds: Lessons Learned from the Kresge HBCU Initiative,* notes that at the end of the program, the five grantees had improved their fundraising capabilities significantly and greatly increased the level of support they raised from private sources.[17] This program clearly illustrates how essential it is for an organization to have a solid infrastructure to lead its fundraising efforts.

Consider your organization fortunate if you have the resources to hire a fundraising professional. Not every organization, particularly those serving black communities, is in the financial position to hire a dedicated fundraiser. The median salary for a fundraising professional in the United States with a bachelor's degree and 6–8 years of experience is $76,679.[18] The cost for a fundraising consultant depends on the specific needs of the organization; however, for a reputable consulting firm, the cost can vary from between $500 to $1,250 per day. Some consultants will charge by the hour with rates likely to be around $100 to $125 per hour, which will add up to about $1,000 per day.[19]

Therefore, the question often arises, "Can a nonprofit organization hire fundraisers and compensate them based on a percentage of what they raise?" According to the *Code of Ethical Principals and Standards of Professional Practice*[20] adopted by the Association of Fundraising Professionals (AFP), fundraisers are *not* allowed to take a percentage of what they raise. Standard #12 states, "Members shall not accept compensation that is based on a percentage of contributions; nor shall they accept finder's fees."[21] In addition, Standard #9 states, "Members shall take care to ensure that contributions are used in accordance with the donors' intentions."[22] If a fundraiser charges an organization a fee of 10 percent on what he raises and he solicits a $1,000 contribution from an individual, then he would expect to receive compensation in the amount of $100. However, in the interest of full disclosure, that donor should be asked if he is agreeable to $100 of his $1,000 contribution being paid to the fundraiser for his services. If he agrees, then only $900 of his contribution is tax-deductible.

Explore these options more fully before deciding which is best for your organization.

Empowering the Effective Fundraiser

Empowering an *effective* fundraiser is essential to the strength and credibility of an organization. Some of the same principles that allow for-profit companies to succeed are also at play in the nonprofit world—and ultimately, success depends on the quality and experience of their people. That depth of experience is reflected in how well the people at the organization know their customer. In the nonprofit world, the customer is the donor—and all efforts by the fundraiser should focus on understanding his or her motivations. Notes Alice Green Burnette:[23] "The fundraiser who focuses on the needs and interests of prospects and donors will raise more money than the fundraiser who focuses primarily on the needs of his or her organization."[24]

Clearly, then, an effective fundraiser is one who can connect with his or her prospect by forging a relationship of mutual respect that comes from listening and understanding the donor's needs, experiences, and interests. The ability to then demonstrate how the nonprofit organization's priorities align with those interests—identifying how the organization can meet the donor's needs and not the other way around—is fundamental to establishing a successful, and potentially long-term, donor relationship. Central to this process is clear and consistent communication on the part of the fundraiser—staying true to the mission of the organization while finding ways to communicate that are best suited to the donor's frame of reference. In this way, the effective fundraiser does not "sell" the priorities of the nonprofit, but rather explores and communicates a common conviction that potentially exists between the donor prospect and the nonprofit.[25]

African American Fundraisers

As in any new relationship, a fundraiser's ability to connect with a potential donor can be directly related to the backgrounds and experiences of each individual. It's perfectly acceptable to acknowledge that donor prospects may embrace and trust a fundraiser with whom they can relate. Nonprofits in the African American community should ensure their staff reflects the diversity of their donor population, and that means hiring and cultivating African American fundraising professionals.

While there seems to be a growing number of black professionals in nonprofit roles, there is a noted disparity in their participation in professional organizations such as the Association of Fundraising Professionals (AFP) and in obtaining fundraising credentials such as certification through Certified Fund Raising Executives (CFRE) International, the internationally-recognized fundraising credentialing organization. In fact, black fundraisers make up only 1.2 percent of the fundraising population who have achieved professional certification.[26]

According to Alisa Smallwood, CFRE, Vice President of Development for the Center for Civil and Human Rights and member of the CFRE board, "Not enough black fundraisers have professional certification. This in no way reflects upon our abilities. However, I'm concerned that there isn't a sense of urgency among us to remain engaged in continuing education and professional advancement opportunities. Donors are becoming more sophisticated. And demonstrating our involvement in professional organizations can only help to inspire their confidence in our efforts." When pressed as to why she thinks that black fundraisers are not taking the CFRE exam, she speculated that it's probably not intentional; it's just a matter of priorities and the time that it takes to prepare for the exam is not at the top of many fundraising professionals' to-do list, regardless of color.[27] Several fundraisers shared that in their pursuit of a fundraising position, potential employers placed their emphasis on the number of years a candidate has worked in the profession and the amount of money they have raised, rather than whether they had their CFRE credentials.

So, does this mean that African American fundraising should eschew the credentialing process? The answer, for the following reasons, is no. First of all, the credentialing process ensures that the fundraiser has up-to-date knowledge of the latest techniques that are proving successful (or unsuccessful) in the field; second, credentialing reduces the feeling of isolation and going it alone that is so endemic in fundraising, by linking the person with a network of similarly qualified people who can be called upon, from time to time, to help one think through an issue or for simple moral support; third, future employers in greater numbers will be likely to seek fundraisers with experience enhanced by credentials. And finally, credentialing may result in a more knowledgeable and effective fundraising professional.

Just how many African American fundraisers are there? There may be more than we are aware of because many do not self-identify as fundraising professionals. In the report "African American Development Officers: Confronting the Obstacles and Rising Above Them in the New Millennium,"[28] a large number of the individuals interviewed had one job title but dual responsibilities—often with the second responsibility focused on fundraising. Since their job titles did not reflect their fundraising responsibilities, they did not identify themselves as professional fundraisers. As a result, these individuals did not always participate in professional development opportunities for fundraisers, where they would have been counted among African American fundraising professionals. This was the case more often at smaller organizations.[29]

The nonprofit community would do well to increase, continually and significantly, the number of African Americans who choose a career in fundraising. But how do we ensure that more blacks enter the profession? According to Charles Stephens,[30] author of *Professionalism in Black Philanthropy*, the fault lies with the educational programs available to African Americans who wish to enter the field of philanthropy in general. He asserts that the most significant problem is that, while there are currently 116 historically black colleges and universities in America, not one of those institutions offers programs concentrated on opportunities for careers in philanthropy. This, he said, must change.[31]

The participation of blacks in professional roles in philanthropy creates the balance of insight, perspective, and conviction needed to steward some of the most important missions of nonprofit organizations throughout the nation.[32] Notes Rob Henry, executive director of emerging constituencies with the Council for Advancement and Support of Education (CASE) in a recent article titled "The Diverse Manager" in *Advancing Philanthropy*:

> *People of diverse backgrounds who are in management are often the only ones at the table. How do you become the expert in the organization and create other champions? You have to find others and pull them into the pipeline. You will have a greater voice at the table if there is more than one person with a diverse background. You get to the center of power by bringing more on board.*[33]

Bringing that diverse voice to the table is perhaps most empowering in the management structure of the nonprofit world.[34]

African American Donors

For the African American community, nonprofits can deliver strategies that will cultivate varying philanthropic interests by providing this emergent donor population with a clear message of program goals and measures of accountability. With African Americans now comprising a significant percentage of the donor population, nonprofits, especially those serving the black community, need to understand the cultural differences of this group and engage in strategies that embrace the different giving interests among them. In a report entitled "Nonprofit Performance, Fundraising Effectiveness, and Strategies for Engaging African Americans in Philanthropy" by David M. Van Slyke of Syracuse University and Shena Ashley and Janet L. Johnson of Georgia State University, the authors assert:[35]

> *A standard operating strategy among many resource development specialists is that African Americans as a group are homogeneous in their motivations and preferences for charitable engagement. By*

extension, then, the solicitation methods and incentives to which the African Americans respond to requests from charities must also be the same. This critical misunderstanding results from both in-adequate empirical information about African American philan-thropy and a failure to recognize the diversity within this donor population.[36]

General best practices of fundraising apply to all donors—*regardless of race*—and creating the building blocks of knowl-edge means conducting background research and understand-ing the motivations and experiences that incentivize a donor to give. African Americans identify with other African Amer-icans when it comes to their past, but when it comes to the future they no longer feel obligated to support African Amer-ican causes.[37] This change is having an impact on organiza-tions that have traditionally relied on African Americans to support organizations that focus on traditional civil rights is-sues, even when these organizations have been deficient in the services they provide. No longer can they expect that because "I'm black and you're black" that's reason enough for you to support us.

In "Hopscotching in the Neighborhood," Alice Green Bur-nett uses the child's game as a metaphor for the work that goes into identifying, soliciting, and cultivating an African Amer-ican donor—advising that fundraisers should not skip steps when following the process for effective fundraising. She notes that, as in hopscotch, a fundraiser should "navigate sequen-tially" and acknowledges: "It takes a lot of skill and dexterity in order to win—at hopscotch and at fundraising in the Black community."[38]

Nonprofits, then, need to ensure that their own fundraisers are educated, informed, and prepared (credentialed?) to address the particular nuances of the black community and the cultural dimensions that impact giving.

Unrestricted Funds: The Lifeblood of the Nonprofit Organization

An experienced fundraiser knows how important unrestricted funds are to the strength of the nonprofit organization. Donors, however, have a tendency to prefer to direct their giving toward a specific program or project; often, it's because they want to believe their gift has a direct impact on something tangible or measurable. In transitioning from traditional church and community-based giving practices, African American donors are particularly concerned with the impact of their money. A report on African American giving produced by the Community Foundation of Greater Atlanta stated:

> *African American philanthropists hold themselves to high levels of responsibility to ensure meaningful contributions, or "giving well." Nonprofit organizations would do well to assist the African American to "cultivate the philanthropist within" by addressing the issues of responsible giving.*[39]

Thus, an effective fundraising strategy will cultivate its fundraisers in a manner that equips them to translate effectively the impact of a donor's money—and that includes conveying how critical unrestricted funds are to an organization.

By effectively conveying organizational impact that is successful to individuals, a nonprofit is tapping into the largest and most powerful pool of donors in America. According to the 2008 report produced by the Giving USA Foundation, individuals are the most generous of the donor populations.[40] So while there are often more dimensions and nuances to take into account when soliciting individuals as donors, the success of the nonprofit and its ability to fulfill its mission is all but reliant on this group of philanthropists.

If You Fail to Plan, You Plan to Fail

Regardless of the color of the donor or the organization, it is essential to have a basic fundraising plan in order to position yourself for success. Whether your organization needs to raise a large or small amount of money, it's important to develop a basic and effective fundraising plan. Typically, the plan will identify a small number of prospects (that is, potential donors) with significant means and how to cultivate (that is, "pursue" them), rather than try to reach as many prospects as possible. Later on, the fundraising plan can be expanded to create a long-term fundraising plan that will include more potential donors to continue the funding stream and build upon your organization's work. There are many opportunities in your community to get low cost or free assistance with your organization's fundraising. Check in with the local major fundraising consulting firms (even some of the national ones) and find out if they offer pro bono assistance to nonprofit organizations—many of them do. You can also check local foundations and find the ones that offer technical assistance grants or grants that support hiring a fundraising consultant. There are hundreds of organizations that provide assistance to nonprofit organizations such as the Alliance for Nonprofit Management, which is the professional association of individuals and organizations devoted to improving the management and governance capacity of nonprofits, and the Georgia Center for Nonprofits, which is Georgia's association for nonprofit, charitable organizations.

Its mission is to serve, strengthen, and support Georgia's non-profit community.

Call to Action: Innovative Ways to Raise Money

Your organization has planned, strategized, and organized. You have a solid fundraising plan and a person dedicated to implementing that plan. Your fiscal audit can stand the scrutiny of any grantmaker, prospective donor, or board member. Your organization is credible by the strictest of standards, yet you still find it difficult to land those large gifts that your organization so desperately needs. It's time to think of new and innovative ways to reach your audience. Following are some examples.

Build Strategic Alliances! Like the United Negro College Fund, which began as a united effort in 1943 with 27 historically black colleges and universities and collectively raised $760,000 ($8.6 million today),[41] a merger between organizations with common objectives can have tremendous success.[42] Pooling resources can raise an organization's visibility, increase its effectiveness, and attract support for its cause. Planning a successful alliance is critical. The following eight steps will help:

1. **Start Small.** Start with an event or workshop with one partner. After you've gained experience you can team up with two or more partners at a time.
2. **Identify Potential Partners.** Make a list of potential partners. Look for those whose missions are compatible. Don't automatically pick an organization you already know well.
3. **Create a Statement of Purpose.** Explain why your organization wants to form an alliance in terms of your individual

organization. *The more in harmony your organization is with your partner the more successful your partnership will be.*

4. **Jointly Establish Short-Term Goals.** Create measurable and attainable concrete goals.

5. **Be Sensitive to Each Organization's Long-Term Goals.** Each organization should know what the other organization's long-term goals are and respect them.

6. **Identify Responsibilities.** Clearly outline each organization's responsibilities.

7. **Define How to Resolve Conflicts.** Form a small committee from both organizations. This committee will oversee the alliance's operation.

8. **Build on Success.** Any nonprofit can find areas in which pooling resources makes sense. Joint efforts will help your organization, your partner's, and the entire nonprofit sector.

Motivate people to form Giving Circles, a form of philanthropy consisting of groups of individuals who pool their funds and other resources to donate to their communities and seek to increase their awareness and engagement in the process of giving. The circles can serve as a form of shared, or collective, giving in the context of community economic development or other social ventures. Members of giving circles donate their own money or time to a pooled fund, decide together where to give these away, and often have some sort of social or educational interaction associated with the giving. Many circles, in addition to donating their money, also contribute their time and skills to supporting local causes. Donations may range from spare change to thousands of dollars each year. The Change Fund is a giving circle for young African American professionals in the Baltimore area, designed to expand their involvement in philanthropy and to further awareness of social issues. In 2007 members of the Fund had raised $12,000 to support organizations working to improve access, education, and leadership among African American youth in Maryland.

Call on professionals to donate their time such as the Development Assistance Project, which is an example of professionals pooling their talent and resources to assist organizations in their community. The Development Assistance Project was established by the African-American Development Officers Network (AADO). AADO is one of approximately a dozen organizations around the country comprised of African American professionals that have designated fundraising as their primary responsibility in their organization. The mission of the network is to foster professional development and facilitate interaction among members. The AADO Development Assistance Project was started in an effort to provide assistance to area nonprofits that don't have the expertise or the resources to fundraise. Organizations applying must have a budget of less than $1 million and cannot have a fulltime professional fundraiser. AADO selects two organizations per year, and two teams of professionals (approximately 10 on each team) meet with these organizations to design a fundraising plan and provide assistance with implementing it. The team works with the organization for a full year. Any network of professionals can offer the same assistance in their community.

Continue to think innovatively and share what is successful!

Is Your Nonprofit's Story One of Success?

Imagine yourself stepping on the elevator of a major hotel and Oprah Winfrey is already on. She notices your folder bulging with materials, reads the name of your organization on the cover, and asks "What does your organization do?" You have 90 seconds to tell her where your organization has been, where it is today, where it is headed in the future, and what it will cost to get there. If you are so fortunate as to be on that elevator, would you be able to provide a succinct yet compelling case to Oprah—one that not only illuminates the value of the work you're doing, but creates a sense of urgency that reflects how important philanthropic support will be to achieving your program goals? If you have been diligent in developing a detailed fundraising plan, it will reflect in your confidence and readiness to present your case at any moment, in any circumstance.

When Our Nonprofits Are Successful, Our Community Benefits

Healthy nonprofit organizations continue to be fundamental to our achievement and progress as a black community. Our organizations inspire potential donors because of their mission, but remember that potential donors need more than that to be moved to give; effective fundraising is a critical piece of the puzzle. Potential donors will decide to make an investment in our organizations because we stay true to our mission; we strategically plan our fundraising work; we invest in a skilled fundraising leader; we are accountable to our constituents; and we are fiscally sound. With this foundation, our nonprofit organizations are well-poised for success and when our organizations are successful our Community is strengthened.

Notes

1. S. Bond, Press Release (June 23, 2008). Available from Giving USA Foundation: www.givingusa.org/press_releases/releases/20080622.html.

2. Ibid.

3. Ibid.

4. Ibid.

5. Ibid.

6. Amy Blackwood, K. T. Wing, and T. H. Pollack, *The Non Profit Sector in Brief* (May 2008). Retrieved June 2008, from National Center for Charitable Statistics—Urban Institute: http://nccsdataweb.urban.org/kbfiles/797/Almanac2008publicCharities.pdf.

7. L. M. Salamon, *Nonprofits and Development: The Challenge and the Opportunity* (July 12, 1996). Available at Issues of Democracy: http://usinfo.state.gov/journals/itdhr/0198/ijde/salamon.htm.

8. Blackwood, Wing, and Pollack, *The Non Profit Sector in Brief.*

9. *Roots That Run Deep: An Historical Look at the Impact of the United Negro College Fund and its Member Colleges on American History* (n.d.). United Negro College Fund: www.uncf.org/doc/UNCF_Impact_History.pdf.

10. L. M. Salamon, *Nonprofits and Development: The Challenge and the Opportunity* (July 12, 1996). Available at Issues of Democracy: http://usinfo.state.gov/journals/itdhr/0198/ijde/salamon.htm.

11. Ibid.

12. G. Hora, *Cultural Dimensions of Fundraising* (St. Paul: The First Monday Report-Office of Lutheran Campus Ministry Advancement, 2006).

13. Emmett D. Carson, Ph.D., is internationally recognized as a catalyst for progressive social change. A renowned speaker, he has published more than 75 works on philanthropy and social justice. Carson served for 12 years as president and CEO of The Minneapolis Foundation and currently serves as the first CEO and president of the Silicon Valley Community Foundation. He received his M.A. and Ph.D. in public administration in public and international affairs from Princeton University after earning a bachelor's degree in economics, Phi Beta Kappa, from Morehouse College.

14. E. D. Carson, "Black Philanthropy's Past Present, and Future," *Wiley InterScience Journals* 48 (2005).

15. B. S. Schulze, "Changing the Odds: Lessons Learned from the Kresge HBCU Initiative," *Chronicle of Philanthopy* (2005).

16. Ibid.

17. Ibid.

18. *Average Fundraising Manager Salary.* (2008). Available from Salary. Com—Career Advancement Tools and Resources: http://swz .salary.com/salarywizard/layouthtmls/swzl_compresult_national_ FA06000564.html.

19. T. Poderis, *Consulting Agreement for an Annual Campaign* (2008). Available from Fund-Raising Forum: www.raise-funds.com/012202 forum.html.

20. *Ethics* (2001). Available from Association of Fundraising Professionals: www.afpnet.org/ethics.

21. Ibid.

22. Ibid.

23. Alice Green Burnette (1943–2006) worked for 42 years in the advancement field and was the Principal of Advancement Solutions. She served as Assistant Secretary for Institutional Advancement at the Smithsonian Institution. Previously, she served as Director of Development at both Morehouse College and Howard University. She authored a handbook for fundraising professionals, "The Privilege to Ask." In 2003, she co-authored "Achieving Excellence in Fund Raising," which set the standards for fund raising professionals.

24. A. G. Burnette, "Hopscotching in the Neighborhood," *New Directions for Philanthropic Fundraising* (Summer 2005): 113–122.

25. Ibid.

26. *CFRE Fast Facts* (2007). Available from CFRE International, www.cfre.org/cfre-fast-facts.html.

27. Ibid.

28. B. S. Burton, *African American Development Officers: Confronting the Obstacles and Rising Above them in the New Millennium.* (Washington, D.C.: Association of Fundraising Professionals, 2005).

29. Ibid.

30. Charles R. Stephens is Senior Consultant, Partner, and Director with consulting firm Skystone Ryan. Stephens was national chairman of the Association of Fundraising Professionals, which initiated the Charles R. Stephens Excellence in Diversity Award in recognition of his outstanding leadership. Before joining Skystone Ryan, his professional career included positions as chief development officer/vice president with Indiana University's prestigious Center on

Philanthropy, Clark Atlanta University, Morehouse College and The College Fund/UNCF. He is a graduate of Morehouse College and earned his Master's degree from Central Michigan University.

31. Stephens, C. R. "Professionalism in Black Philanthropy: We Have a Chance to Get it Right," *New Directions for Philanthropic Fundraising* (2005, Summer): 13–19.

32. J. P. Boice, "The Diverse Manager," *Advancing Philanthropy* (March/April 2007).

33. Ibid.

34. Ibid.

35. David M. Van Slyke, S. A. *Nonprofit Performance, Fundraising Effectiveness, and Strategies for Engaging African Americans in Philanthropy* (Atlanta: Sage Publications, 2007).

36. Ibid.

37. Carson, "Black Philanthropy's Past Present, and Future."

38. Burnette, "Hopscotching in the Neighborhood," 113–122.

39. *Giving: A Shared Inheritance, African American Giving & Volunteering in Metro Atlanta* (Atlanta: The Community Foundation for Greater Atlanta, 2005).

40. S. Bond, Press Release (June 23, 2008). Available from Giving USA Foundation: www.givingusa.org/press_releases/releases/20080622.html.

41. *Our History* (2007). Available from United Negro College Fund: www.uncf.org/history/default.asp.

42. D.Remley, *Nonprofit World: Pool Resources for Success* (1998). Available from BNET.COM.

Chapter 4

Youth in Philanthropy

Jeanette M. Davis-Loeb
Founder and CEO, Rising Oak Foundation, Vashon Island, WA

The Facts on Youth in Philanthropy

Power in Numbers

- An estimated 15.5 million youth or 55 percent of youth, ages 12 to 18, participate in volunteer activities; the teen volunteering rate is nearly twice the adult volunteering rate of 29 percent.[1]
- Youth contribute more than 1.3 billion hours of community service each year.[2]
- The typical youth volunteer contributes 29 hours per year, while adult volunteers typically serve 52 hours per year.[3]
- Thirty-nine percent of teen volunteers are "regular" volunteers, defined as those who volunteer at least 12 weeks per year. That compares with 55 percent of adult volunteers who can be classified as "regular."[4]

- Seventy percent of young people ages 15–21 have participated in activities to help strengthen their community at some point in their lives.[5]

Economic and Social Capital

- Seventy-three percent of America's 60 million young people believe they can make a difference in their communities.[6]
- Teenage service is worth $34.3 billion to the U.S. economy.[7]
- Youth who volunteer just one hour a week are 50 percent less likely to abuse drugs, alcohol, or cigarettes, or engage in destructive behavior.[8]
- Youth who volunteer are three times more likely to volunteer as adults.[9]
- The value of service carried out on National Youth Service Day exceeds $171 million.[10]

An Academic Endeavor

- Youth who volunteer are more likely to do well in school, graduate, vote, and be philanthropic.[11]
- Fifty-five percent of those enrolled in school participate in volunteer activities, compared to 26 percent of those not enrolled in school.[12]
- An estimated 10.6 million students nationwide, or 38 percent of students between the ages of 12 and 18, have participated in school-based service, which is defined as community service that takes place as part of a school activity or requirement.[13]
- Sixty-five percent of youth who participate in service as part of a school activity are also engaged in the service-learning–related activities of planning and/or writing about the service project in class.[14]
- Students who attend private schools are 55 percent more likely than students in public schools to participate in

school-based service, and students attending private religious schools are the most likely to participate in school-based service.[15]

Racial Disparities

- Only 17 percent of African American youth are considered "regular" volunteers, working on average just over an hour per week.[16]
- 40.70 percent of black youth don't volunteer at all, as compared to 29.13 percent of white youth.[17]
- An estimated 72.57 percent of African American parents do not volunteer, as opposed to 53.58 percent of white parents.[18]
- Although 68.5 percent of black youth believe that government should do more to solve community problems, only 18.4 percent of them believe that government is responsive to the genuine needs of the public.[19]
- 60.91 percent of African American youth believe that they can personally make a difference but as a rule 40.61 percent of them don't feel that "people" can be trusted. The statistics for white youth are 58.37 percent and 53.17 percent respectively.[20]

Everybody can be great, because anybody can serve. You don't have to have a college degree to serve. You don't have to make your subject and your verb agree to serve. You only need a heart full of grace. A soul generated by love.

—Dr. Martin Luther King, Jr.

If time is a treasure, then making it count is a talent. More simply put, if we value our energy, then sharing it is a gift. Volunteerism, anybody's and everybody's gift, is one of our first opportunities to foster a sense of community ownership, commitment to others, and self-pride within our children. Providing our young people with the knowledge, skills, and right attitude they need to be service leaders is our next best hope for securing the future we wish to see.

For far too long we have tried to shelter our babies from the burdens of past storms, like ignorance, racism, and economic dearth. Altruistically, as loving black parents our cultural motivation was to provide a better beginning for our children. And as a result, our desire to give more became hope put into action; galvanized by the strong belief that through hard work, perseverance, and the profound power of our minds we could positively affect the life trajectory and outcomes for our kids. We purposefully and tirelessly labored for our offspring, so that they wouldn't have to slave to acquire the social and economic successes that generations of our ancestors literally toiled in the fields to achieve.

Unfortunately, that noble ambition, which kept us focused and striving as a people, has not been so easy to attain. Nor has it nurtured within the hearts and psyches of our children the true feelings of entitlement and self-worth, the ultimate gifts of our hard work.

Quite frankly, for many of us, that better beginning we hoped to create became synonymous with the insulation, overindulgence, and outright gentrification of our kids.

By giving, giving, and giving things, we have unintentionally placed the focus on materialism instead of character development and what the spirit brings. We've failed to consistently share that giving and receiving are two sides of the same coin; thereby missing a perfect opportunity to model that success isn't defined by what you have and keep, but by what you have and give to others. Saddened and stunned, we look on as the potential of many of our young people, our sweetest fruit, gradually wither on the vine. With our flawed intentions leading our familial aspirations, we have come to realize that we've overlooked the most critical and fundamental first step: the inclusion of our children in the achievement of the dream.

We have done our young people a grave disservice and made a potential mess of things. By not involving them in the process, we've literally created a generation of takers, who for the most part believe that they are supposed to receive everything without giving anything. The most tragic part of this paradigm is that in their hearts they feel unworthy and undeserving, but don't know why. We could tell them that it's because they didn't earn it; but through no fault of their own, there's no way for them to have simply known how to strive and earn, because we didn't show them or teach them how to take the first step.

A quality work ethic and strong values aren't developed in a vacuum; they are developed and nurtured over time. Therefore, when people aren't asked or expected to give, not only do they lose the joy of receiving; they begin to just take. This paraphrased maxim applies to all of us but especially to our kids. We have to stop saying in words and deeds that they can't rely on themselves. We have to stop saying that they aren't spiritually powerful enough to be what they need to be, or to initiate the change they want to see. We imply, by not asking for their participation and input, that they lack the intellectual capacity to collaborate and lead. We imply that they should wait for someone else to define and create their possibilities, because they lack the attention span to achieve on their own. We unthinkingly continue to diminish their ability to act and advocate for themselves. Then, we wonder why our next generation continues to unravel and turn inward on itself.

At this juncture, it's time for us to deal with the repercussions of our all-consuming love, and the problematic truth that some of our historical successes have become mixed blessings. The existence of black affluence in the midst of black scarcity, social acceptance of some at the expense of social exclusion of others, and the presence of unimaginable hope in the face of complete and total despair are just a few obvious examples of this dichotomy. The plaguing reality of these contrasting truths has made it difficult for us to articulate the intricate nature of our current situation, and properly prepare our young people to be of service, not just to us but to the world as well.

Having said that, our immediate challenge is to find a way to release our children from the antiquated model we've tied them to. For clearly, this form of false entitlement does not work, nor does it affirm our young people in the way we intended. We've obviously taken some wrong turns, but all that means is that our journey has been a bit longer. If we are willing to regroup and take a different direction, we can empower our young people to lead in the present and the future, by providing them with the knowledge, wisdom, and heart they need.

One by one, our children can begin to appreciate that giving and receiving are gifts that transform not just the giver but the receiver as well, from the inside out. They can begin to experience the real-life connection between their acts of service, and the improved quality of life of those they serve locally, nationally, and around the world. Yes, the positive effects of their actions can be far-reaching, and as parents, we can facilitate this shift by making a conscious decision to teach, model, and create opportunities for our children to practice "giving to receive" at home.

Being a service leader is actually fun and personally rewarding, and the ways in which you can involve your children are limitless. Although our kids don't generally have many treasures, they often have plenty spare time, and an unusual array of hidden talents to unearth and explore. I would suggest beginning with their free times and talents as your starting place, since it always seems to be easier to get our young people on board for something they already enjoy doing. To get you going, here are some of the activities my kids have done with me and other members of our community.

Time
- Planting flowers at the local YMCA.
- Stuffing envelopes for the community arts organization.
- Spending time listening, sharing, and even giving manicures and pedicures at the neighborhood nursing home.

Talent
- Performing Storytelling Concerts to raise money for a charity of their choice.
- Participating in a concert with fellow harp students to fundraise for an area nonprofit, that provides resources for homeless youth.

Treasures
- Instead of just another toy for Christmas, receiving a "gift card" to spend through Heifer International. (Heifer International provides farm animals to families around the world as part of its mission to end world hunger and poverty and to care for the Earth.) Learn more at www.heifer.org/.

Leadership requires practice, and these are the baby steps our children will need to take in order to learn, and gain ownership of the philanthropic process. By changing behaviors today we are planting seeds for tomorrow and serving our next generation of leaders in a way that is worthy of who we are, and who we have been. Together, let us continue to nurture and develop the centerpiece of our collective humanity, our young people; for this is truly how the garden will blossom and grow.

What the Philanthropic Community Can Do

How will philanthropists inspire members of the next generation to embrace the call to serve and to ensure that they have the knowledge, skills, and right attitudes to do so strategically and effectively? Here are ways to facilitate that eventuality by teaching, modeling, and creating opportunities for children to discover and harness the power of philanthropy.

Encourage

There are few philanthropic boot camp programs for young people, in communities of color. Why not say, "Philanthropy is for you too," by piloting programs that promote the development of service leaders instead of service receivers, in neighborhoods where such efforts would be gratefully and graciously received.

Educate

Young people have to learn about philanthropy and its critical role in our communities and our society. That means getting the subject of philanthropy into the schools, into after-school programs, youth-serving organizations, and even religious classes.[21]

Model

National organizations have to take the lead in making a commitment to involve young people in their philanthropic work. Once the commitment has been made, they must develop specific programs and resources that can be delivered to state or local chapters, and embark on an ongoing effort to encourage local chapters to involve youth as volunteers in their programs, as donors and fundraisers, and as participants in their governance.[22]

Facilitate

Young people have to be given opportunities to take on their own projects and experience what it means to make a difference.[23]

Validate

Affirm the economic, political, and social value of our young people by duplicating their philanthropic accomplishments and ingenuity. If it can be done well in one black community, it can be done well in another. Here is an opportunity to tell our young people, "excellent work," by providing a vehicle with which they can lead by example and share their experiences with peer groups nationally.

What the Larger Community Can Do

Some say the greatest gift of any community is its ability to nurture and support its youth. Well if that is the case, we have well and truly fallen down on the job, and it is time for us to get right back up. Historically, philanthropy is nothing new in the Black community. More often than not, it has been the word *philanthropy* itself and defining it by the standards of others that has caused some confusion for our folks. So it's not even that we don't know what to do; we're just not doing it; at least not in a way that touches the lives of almost everyone—particularly the lives of all our kids.

A Philanthropic Covenant with Black America

Through common acts of kindness and sustaining our local institutions we've been giving and loving each other for centuries. Baking cakes to raise money for the church, feeding strangers and raising barns are just a few of the many acts of service we've bestowed upon one another. Honestly, had it not been for our propensity to take care of our own, we probably wouldn't have survived as a people for this long. So tell me, whatever happened to "what's mine is yours" and serving strangers as if they were family or close friends? When did we forget that you and me, we, were the community, and start looking to outside sources to fix what was ailing our communal body from within?

We are at a pivotal place in time where we simply don't have another child to lose, especially not another black boy. It's time we take back our power, people, and do what's right for each other. How many more of our children are we going to throw away, because we are too tired or because we expect to be given everything? What in the world! It is truly time to take our lives, families and communities back.

Unfortunately through cultural assimilation, passing the buck, and moving up economically and socially we've lost our footing. Those who stayed want to put it on those who moved away to fix what we see as wrong in our communities, but let's be clear. It is the responsibility of each and every one of us to help heal our communities, because whether we live in the inner city or suburbia, the pain is something we all feel.

When was the last time you volunteered at your church, spent some time at a nursing home loving on some of our elders, or even watched a neighbor's kid until a parent got home from work? When did we stop building each other up? When did we stop giving to receive? We don't have time to wait around for some organization to do the things that we can do for ourselves.

That is too much like waiting for your captor to save you, and of that surely we've had enough. Our community organizations are there to help structure our combined activities and efforts, not to play mammy to some spoon-fed kids.

What we need to do is take responsibility for our actions and those of our children, including our neighbor's kids. Everyone is tired, so that is nothing more than an excuse. If you don't know where to begin, then ask. That too, would be just another excuse. No one owes us anything, so it is entirely up to you and me to produce. We are each a crucial and substantive part of our community: formed when we come together as individuals, hoping to do great and amazing things. What we do separately only gets better when we join forces. It's called combined giving. "Me" is transformed into "we," and becomes the most life-affirming part. So from someone who is sitting in the same boat, and who is willing to continue bailing with you to stay afloat, I ask that you do just one thing. Pick one way that you can give, and do it today. And while you're at it, don't forget to bring your kids.

What Every Individual Can Do Now

A philanthropic nature like a loving one is nurtured within the home. As an intrinsic part of our everyday lives, we are blessed to share the challenges and victories of "giving to receive." Here are a few simple ways to plant the seeds of service, commitment, and pride within our kids.

- Especially as a parent, lead by example and become a volunteer.
- Give of your heart, mind, and spirit. Share all of the gifts and talents with which the Lord has blessed you.
- Ask and expect our young people to join us in serving.

- Mentor in your community. Teach and model good stewardship, divine and otherwise.
- Create age- and skill-appropriate opportunities for young people to give.
- Empower our next generation to take the lead and create the positive changes they want to see.
- Receive the joy of giving and pass it on.

What Works Now

Michigan Women's Foundation: Young Women for Change Program

Young Women for Change (YWFC) is a group of young women, ages 14–18, of diverse backgrounds, who assess the needs of local girls and young women, and grant funds to nonprofit organizations working to serve girls and young women in their local communities.

Learn more at www.miwf.org/movie(1024x768).html.

Student African American Brotherhood

The Student African American Brotherhood Organization is a dynamic organization established specifically to assist our participants to excel academically, socially, culturally, professionally, and in the community. SAAB is primarily comprised of male students who strive for academic excellence and make a commitment to plan and implement programs that benefit their community at large. We encourage our participants to embrace leadership by being positive examples for each other through a strong commitment to academic achievement, brotherhood, and community service. We provide weekly study sessions, weekly developmental seminars for students of all ages, business meetings, social and religious activities, and work with various nonprofit service agencies (such as Habitat for Humanity, Big Brothers and Big Sisters, Boys Club, and so on). Learn more at www.2cusaab.org/index.htm.

The Young Leaders' Academy of Baton Rouge, Inc.

The Young Leaders' Academy of Baton Rouge, Inc. exists to nurture the development of leadership abilities of young African American males, empowering them to improve the quality of their lives and assist them in becoming productive citizens. One of our core objectives is to develop within our young men an appreciation and lifelong commitment to service. Learn more at www.youngleaders.org/our_faces.htm.

Associated Black Charities of Maryland

Associated Black Charities is a Maryland-based nonprofit organization that cultivates, secures, and directs financial and intellectual capital toward developing self-sustaining, cooperative, and competitive communities through responsible leadership, investment, and philanthropy. Learn more at www.abc-md.org/.

Association of Black Foundation Executives (ABFE)

ABFE promotes effective and responsive philanthropy in black communities by growing black leadership and participation within organized philanthropy, enhancing the effectiveness of philanthropic leaders and institutions that fund and invest in black communities, and increasing the allocation of philanthropic resources that address priority issues in black communities. Learn more at www.abfe.org/.

The National Center for Black Philanthropy

The Mission of the National Center is to promote giving and volunteerism among African Americans, foster full participation by African Americans in all aspects of philanthropy, educate the public about the contributions of black philanthropy, strengthen people and institutions engaged in black philanthropy, and research the benefits of black philanthropy to all Americans. Learn more at www.blackphilanthropy.org/.

> *. . . we also rejoice in our sufferings, because we know that suffering produces perseverance; perseverance, character; and character, hope.*
> —Romans 5:3-4

Our blessings as a nation lie in inspiring new stewards to embrace the call to serve spiritually, socially, and economically. It simply takes the desire and will to rekindle that once bright light called faith. Having said that, if we as elders take the lead and hold ourselves accountable, we can reconnect with our legacy and help develop the black leaders that our country needs, and so richly deserves. Remember that our most profound breakthroughs occur during our greatest challenges, so model the process, teach perseverance, and celebrate the successes with love.

Notes

1. "Building Active Citizens: The Role of Social Institutions in Teen Volunteering," Brief 1 in the Youth Helping America series. Corporation for National and Community Service, November 2005. Available at www.nationalservice.gov/pdf/05_1130_LSA_YHA_study.pdf.
2. Ibid.
3. Ibid.
4. Ibid.

5. "Do Something: Young People's Involvement Survey." Princeton Survey Research, 1998.

6. Ibid.

7. Independent Sector/Gallup, 1999 Value of Service.

8. Search Institute, 1995.

9. Independent Sector/Gallup, 1999 Value of Service.

10. Youth Service America estimates based on Independent Sector Value of Service, 1999.

11. UCLA/Higher Education Research Institute, 1991.

12. "Building Active Citizens."

13. Ibid.

14. Ibid.

15. Ibid.

16. "Building Active Citizens."

17. Marni Deborah Schultz, "Volunteer Behavior of Minority Youth" (April 2006). Available at http://aladinrc.wrlc.org/bitstream/1961/3644/1/etd_mds66.pdf.

18. Ibid.

19. Civic Engagement among Minority Youth, The Center for Information & Research on Civic Learning & Engagement, 2007. Available online at www.civicyouth.org/PopUps/FactSheets/FS_07_minority_ce.pdf.

20. Marni Deborah Schultz, "Volunteer Behavior of Minority Youth."

21. Statements are from an interview with Patricia O. Bjorhovde, CFRE, and former Chair of Association of Fundraising Professionals Youth in Philanthropy Task Force, by Tom Watson, writer for Today's Fundraiser, see Teaching Philanthropy: Focus on Youth, Today's Fundraiser, 2003. Available at www.afpnet.org/ka/ka-3.cfm?content_item_id=11347&folder_id=3274.

22. Ibid.

23. Ibid.

Chapter 5

Civic Engagement in the African American Community

Stephanie Robinson, Esq.
Founding President and CEO, The Jamestown Project,
New Haven, CT

Charisse Carney–Nunes
Senior Vice-President of Knowledge Development & Media Relations,
The Jamestown Project, New Haven, CT

"The most important political office is that of the private citizen."[1] While the wisdom of these simple words that Justice Louis Brandeis wrote is apparent, the path to realizing this aspiration eludes American democracy to this day. As we create this historic Philanthropic Covenant with Black America, Chapter 5 considers how the philanthropic community can advance civic engagement to inspire ordinary Americans to become active and engaged around realizing the agenda set forth in the Covenant with Black America.

Civic Engagement Defined

Civic engagement is defined as individual or collective actions designed to identify and address issues of public concern. It occurs when inspired people and organizations not only *view* themselves as agents of change, but also *act* upon that view. Civic engagement can take a variety of forms from volunteering in a soup kitchen to volunteering in a political campaign, from participation in a neighborhood association to writing a letter to an elected official. And voting, of course, is one of the most apparent forms of civic engagement, though not the only form. Inspiring and training ordinary people to become agents of the change they seek are sure ways for foundations to create increased social value from their investments. But civic engagement is much more than an intelligent investment strategy; a citizenry engaged in civic action, we think, is a necessary component to any philanthropic strategy to cure any societal ill.

As students of American jurisprudence one of our earliest lessons in democracy was the study of Alexis de Tocqueville, a French civil servant from an aristocratic family, who wrote the now-famous text *Democracy in America* following a nine-month visit to the United States in 1831–1832. Tocqueville sought to understand and analyze the potential of the American democratic experiment as a context from which to draw on his own political aspirations in France. His observations speak volumes about the importance of civic engagement in America.

Tocqueville observed that the tendency of American citizens to organize themselves in private associations was a critical underpinning of American democracy. He wrote, "In no

94

country in the world has the principle of association been more successfully used or applied to a greater multitude of objects than in America. Besides the permanent associations which are established by law under the names of townships, cities, and counties, a vast number of others are formed and maintained by the agency of private individuals."[2] Tocqueville viewed this American "habit" of forming ourselves into deliberative bodies of "thinking men" to be crucial to the success of democracy here. He saw this kind of civic engagement of citizens as a necessary guarantee required in any democracy to protect against the tyranny of the majority or the exercise of arbitrary power by the elected or other elites.[3]

But what would Tocqueville think of a disengaged citizenry in America? What if he had observed nonthinking men and women who had little time or inclination to involve themselves in their communities? What if these nonthinking citizens participated in democracy through voting but then refrained from engaging in the other forms of activity that Tocqueville viewed as critical to guard against the elected majority's abuse of power? If the French aristocrat were to visit America today, would he write an exhaustive treatise extolling the virtues of our democracy, or would he observe a democracy in peril?

The answers to these questions are unclear. In general, recent decades have shown a sharp decline in civic engagement in America. Voter participation, volunteerism, and even civic club participation have all declined in past decades (generally between the 1960s and 1990s). But the tragic events of September 11, 2001, helped to rebirth a spirit of civic renewal in many Americans. "The Bureau of Labor Statistics reported that 59 million Americans regularly volunteered in the year after 9/11, growing to 63 million two years later and increasing even more [as recently as 2005]."[4] National and international service programs, the Peace Corps, the Red Cross, and countless business and educational service organizations are all enjoying this hopeful civic resurgence.[5] In sum, it appears that civic engagement in America, while enjoying a resurgence, is also in need of strengthening and a broad sustainability plan.

Philanthropy to the Rescue?

Assuming (as we do) that civic engagement is a necessary component to American democracy that needs to be strengthened, one might argue that there can be no better community to revive our democracy than the philanthropic community. *Philanthropy*, which may be defined in many ways, literally comes from the Greek and means "love of mankind." As such, it follows that the philanthropic community in America would prioritize investments that it believed would increase the tendency for citizens to become active and engaged in their communities. But some commentators question whether the philanthropic community can do so.

Identifying the Challenges for Philanthropy

William Schambra, director of the Hudson Institute's Bradley Center for Philanthropy and Civic Renewal, has written extensively about the tension between philanthropy and civic engagement.[6] A critic of sorts, Schambra points to the history of twentieth-century philanthropy in America and its obsession with science, experts, and evaluation and concludes that this "professionalism" has been disabling to citizens and the ordinary voluntary associations that they inhabit.[7] "These developments have brought us to today's moment of peril for American democracy. Our culture today is full of the disabling message that the expert knows better than the citizen."[8]

Schambra continues is critique in an essay in the new book *Giving Well, Doing Good,* in which he questions Warren Buffett's decision to bequeath billions to the "ungodly bright" leaders of the Bill and Melinda Gates Foundation. He challenges American philanthropy's "romance" with the "ungodly bright" among us. He dares the philanthropic community to let go of the notion that "the ungodly bright are somehow better equipped to solve society's problems than are everyday citizens."[9]

In commenting on the philanthropic community's readiness to tackle the challenge of increasing civic engagement, Schambra argues that the community must first ensure that it is, in fact, *for* civic engagement. "Sadly, even when the focus is on civic engagement itself, professionals have subtle ways of insuring that *their* understanding of engagement crowds out that of an everyday citizen."[10] Will the foundation take a chance on a less mature group? Will they respect the work of the amateur group in addressing the particular problem, or will the group be criticized for not dealing with the root cause of the issue?

The Will to Confront the Challenges

The good news is that whatever biases the philanthropic community may have, support for advancing civic engagement is increasing. An informal survey of the websites of top U.S. foundations reveals that a small but growing number have funding strategies that include supporting democracy and civic engagement.[11] There are also a growing number of community foundations supporting more grassroots philanthropy-supporting organizations that may otherwise be overlooked.

A growing number of foundations exist that are developing an interest in the cross-section between civic engagement and philanthropy. Philanthropy for Active Civic Engagement (PACE), for example, is a community of grantmakers and donors committed to strengthening democracy by using the power, influence, and resources of philanthropy to open pathways to participation. In a recent essay published on the organization's website, public policy expert John M. Bridgeland assessed the post-September 11 landscape for civic engagement and philanthropy in America, and concluded that "the time is ripe for civic renewal," and offered the philanthropic community very specific advice on how to get it done.[12]

So, assuming the philanthropic community has the iron will to confront the challenges that Schambra puts forth, and assuming the community is galvanized around the concept of civic philanthropy, what then is the best *strategy* for the community to undertake?

Strategic Philanthropy for Civic Engagement

To the extent that Schambra suggests that the challenges he elucidates may be overcome by large foundations merely opening their doors to more grassroots organizations, we disagree. To the extent one may think that the answer exists solely in the proliferation of community foundations to support the wisdom and the energy of ordinary citizens, we also disagree. While both of these activities are crucial components to a solution to overcome the Schambra challenges, we think what is needed is a comprehensive strategy for the philanthropic community.

Underlying the strategy, we think, is a rejection of the idea that civic engagement and traditional philanthropy are diametrically opposite. We also think that it is instructive to examine the well-documented model of conservative philanthropy.

A 1997 report by the National Committee on Responsive Philanthropy "documented the role that conservative foundations have played in developing and sustaining America's conservative labyrinth."[13] In a three-year period, 12 foundations awarded $210 million to support a wide array of conservative projects and institutions resulting in increased power and influence of the conservative policy movement. The multifaceted approach of this philanthropic strategy certainly had the effect of energizing ordinary Americans inclined to agree with their movement and included the following components:

- Academic Sector Organizations and Programs—to train the next generation of conservative thinkers and activists.
- National Think Tanks and Advocacy Groups—to build a national infrastructure of these organizations focusing on issue areas of importance to the movement.
- Media Groups—to build and solidify the support of ordinary Americans.
- Legal Organizations.
- State and Regional Think Tanks and Advocacy Groups.
- Religious Sector Organizations.
- Philanthropic Institutions and Networks.[14]

So what then are the five key components of a philanthropic strategy that will have the effect of increasing civic engagement, particularly around the Covenant-agenda items?

1. **Strategic Grantmaking.** Chapter 1 of this Covenant examines strategic grantmaking. Glover Blackwell suggests a strategic approach to ensure that more foundation dollars directly reach or benefit the communities they seek to serve.

This analysis recognizes the importance of issue-based philanthropy, while underscoring the need for such funding to be strategic if it is to have the intended impact. We think that strategic grantmaking is a key component of a strategy to utilize philanthropic support to increase civic engagement.

2. **Grassroots Philanthropy.** We also think that foundations *should* fund more grassroots organizations. Well-endowed foundations can "take risks and can afford to fail."[15] Foundations should embrace Tocqueville. They should trust and support citizens in their problem-solving endeavors. Again, this is a key component to a philanthropic strategy for civic engagement.

3. **Democratic Practice.** Additionally, we think foundations should fund *organizations* working to foster and increase civic engagement and democratic practice teaching and inspiring communities to become the agents of change. Such organizations that focus on putting democracy into action should be directed to embed techniques into the labyrinth that create more connected, more responsive communities with the tools to become the agents of change.

4. **Projects to Professionalize Civic Engagement.** We think that support is needed for projects to professionalize civic engagement. Some of Bridgeland's recommendations for civic philanthropy could be particularly instructive here, including his call for supporting the establishment of civic indicators and his call for the philanthropic community to support dialogues within the community on how to strengthen civic philanthropy.[16]

5. **Creating a Progressive Ideas Sector and Agenda.** We find the multifaceted approach of the conservative philanthropic strategy and its ultimate effect of energizing ordinary Americans to be quite compelling. The progressive

ideas community could benefit from a coordinated support strategy that would train the next generation of progressive thinkers and activists; build an infrastructure of think tanks and advocacy groups; invest in media and media transparency; fund legal organizations; support religious organizations; and create working networks of philanthropic institutions.

What's Race Got to Do with It? Black Civic Philanthropy

So how does all of this apply to philanthropy in the black community?

In the context of creating a philanthropic Covenant with Black America, the above analysis is crucial. If the philanthropic community seeks to authentically tackle the agenda items set forth in the Covenant, we think that African American civic engagement must be strengthened as a necessary component of a sustainable solution.

A good starting point in the quest to strengthen African American civic engagement is to first understand the patterns of black philanthropy and civic engagement that define our community today.

Black philanthropy can be defined in the broadest sense of the term. Among other things, it includes individual giving by African Americans; the philanthropic giving strategies of African American foundations; and also the philanthropy of traditional foundations with interests in the black community or in issues impacting communities of color.

Statistics show that African Americans are extremely charitable as a community. Typically, African Americans give 25 percent more of their discretionary income to charity than whites.

Black giving and typical recipient organizations tend to be "rooted in efforts to overcome oppression." African Americans are motivated by those who are close to them, situations they have overcome, and "efforts that make a difference in the daily lives of other African Americans. In many cases, their philanthropy has been a response to discrimination: slavery and segregation in the past; inequality in education and the workplace today."[17]

So what organizations are the benefactors of all this African American generosity? The number one beneficiary is the black church. The tradition of giving "tithes and offerings" dates back to colonial America when free black churches created mutual aid societies committed to healing the ills of American society.[18] Other organizations benefiting from African American giving include historically black colleges and universities, elite social service organizations such as the Links or the Comus Club, and local social service organizations that serve a particular charitable need. Overall, individual African American donors seem to engage in grassroots philanthropy of the kind that Schambra advocates.

There are precious few endowed African American foundations in the United States. In addition to some lesser known celebrity foundations, the Twenty-First Century Foundation (21CF) is the most well-known national foundation that promotes black philanthropy, provides donor education, and makes grants to advance the black community. Like the priorities that emerge from individual African American donors, 21CF funding supports many African American grassroots organizations that otherwise may not be supported by more traditional foundations.

Single-handedly 21CF promotes many of the key components of our above-referenced philanthropic strategy to increase civic engagement: 21CF program areas and initiatives would tend to support Schambra's grassroots philanthropy, and the organization is also taking a leadership role in developing strategic solutions and networks for the philanthropic community to tackle issues facing African Americans. Still, 21CF is but a single, African American foundation. Additionally, their priority areas do not include a special emphasis on civic engagement.

None of this is meant to minimize the importance of traditional foundations to Black Civic Philanthropy. To the contrary, the patterns of support by African American individuals and foundations strongly suggest the dire need for a more comprehensive philanthropic strategy that will increase civic engagement, particularly around the Covenant-agenda items.

By setting forth 10 agenda-items that confront African Americans and all Americans, the Covenant with Black America issued a challenge. While the book set forth a vision of a brighter future for black people, in order to create that future, people who care must take up those challenges with courage, honesty, and strategic planning. As a black community, we must decide if we are going to allow the Crisis in the Village[19] to become an accepted fact of American culture, or if we are going to marshal every resource in our arsenal to fight. The philanthropic sector with its vast networks and financial resources is one such tool in the arsenal. Civic engagement, we would argue, is a necessary piece of the puzzle to create an overall philanthropic strategy.

This movement will require sacrifices. It will require fundamental changes in our thinking and in the thinking of the philanthropic sector. It will require that we all be open to new ideas and new ways of working with one another "to reach for unprecedented levels of collaboration in planning and in action."[20]

But our hard work will bear wonderful fruit—the realization of the dream of a better world that we all seek to create for our children and to teach them to create for themselves.

Facts on Civic Engagement and Philanthropy

Civic Engagement in America Today

- American participation has declined in a variety of social spectrums, from club participation (down 58 percent) to social gatherings.[21]
- The number of volunteer hours per volunteer, a measure indicating a sustained commitment to one organization, declined 10 percent from 1989 to 2000.[22]
- Overall trust in government has decreased from 73 percent in 1958 to 36 percent in 2003.[23]
- Voter participation decreased 14 percent from 1964 to 2000.[24]
- However, in 2004, voter participation increased to 60 percent, the highest percentage since 1968. This gain represents a 6 percent increase since 2000, the highest jump in 50 years.[25]
- In 2006, 26.7 percent of Americans volunteered.[26]
- Since September 11, 2001, civic engagement, especially among young people, has increased. Voting rates by 18-to-24-year-olds increased 23 percent, and studies show a heightened interest in politics and social issues among American youth. [27]

Strategic Philanthropy

- Conservative foundations have engaged in targeted giving that has played a large role in "sustaining America's conservative labyrinth." Twelve major conservative foundations gave away $1 billion from 1985 to 2000, including $300 million in grants and \$210 million in support of conservative policy making and to achieve strategic institutional objectives.[28]

- Media Transparency reports, "Since the 1960s, conservative forces have shaped public consciousness and influenced elite opinion, recruited and trained new leaders, mobilized core constituencies, and applied significant rightward pressure on mainstream institutions, such as Congress, state legislatures, colleges and universities, the federal judiciary and philanthropy itself."[29]

- Conservative foundations also seek to influence national policy by investing in think tanks and other idea-generating organizations. This has resulted in more focused giving; over three-fourths of donated funds were granted to just 18 percent of grantees.[30]

- Giving circles, groups of donors making strategic donations together to maximize financial and social benefits for donors and the recipient charities, have increased in number from "just a handful" in 2000 to 250 or more in 2004. Such groups have donated more than \$400 million.[31]

- More than 800 CEOs have committed to Business Strengthening America, a movement committed to creating institutional changes in the way corporations give by focusing on creating a culture of service in their employees and corporate policies.[32]

Black Giving and Volunteerism

- African Americans give 25 percent more of their discretionary income than whites to philanthropic and charitable organizations.[33]

- African Americans born before the 1960s are more likely to support charitable causes that focus their aid on the black community.[34]

- African Americans born after the 1960s are more likely to support charitable causes that focus their aid on causes that benefit people across races and ethnicities.[35]
- Studies show that African Americans want to support organizations in their local communities rather than organizations sponsored by the government or larger-scale organizations.[36]
- While 79 percent of African Americans age 40 and older volunteered at the organization to which they gave the most money, only 40 percent of African Americans under age 40 volunteered at the organization that received their donations.[37]
- Among African American donors age 40 and older studied by the Center on Philanthropy and Civil Society, 87 percent had organized an event, 95 percent had served on a board, and 26 percent had set up a fund or program.[38]
- Among African American donors under age 40, 70 percent had experience organizing an event, 40 percent had experience serving on a board, and 5 percent had experience setting up a fund or program.[39]
- While only 18 percent of African American donors age 40 and up were specific in their vision for philanthropic giving, 60 percent of younger African American donors were specific in their goals and objectives for philanthropy.[40]
- Motivations for African American donors under age 40 include a strong focus on social change (45 percent of donors) and great attention to educational issues (80 percent).[41]

Black Civic Engagement
- In 2006 19.2 percent of African Americans volunteered.[42]
- In 2004 56.3 percent of blacks voted, while 60.3 percent of whites did so.[43]

- In 2000 and 2004, minority neighborhoods with high poverty had higher percentages of uncounted votes than other communities.[44]
- African American voting increased 11 percent from the 2000 to the 2004 presidential election, constituting the largest increase in voter turnout among any racial or ethnic group of that election cycle.[45]
- In 2003, African American youth were the least likely of any ethnic group to participate in community service, extracurricular activities, or other early indicators of civic engagement.[46]
- In 2006, African Americans ages 15–25 were the most politically-involved ethnic group, most likely to vote regularly, join a political group, and donate money to a political campaign.[47]

What the Philanthropic Community Can Do

The philanthropic community is already beginning to acknowledge the importance of civic engagement as a fundamental strategy in philanthropy. Without active and engaged citizens the charitable goals of nongovernmental organizations will not be realized, and the noble works of such organizations will be in want. The philanthropic community is best positioned to design a multipoint program to tackle the issues set forth in the Covenant. The points of the program relating to civic engagement are summarized above in our introductory essay. The proposed action steps for getting it done are summarized below:

- **Step One: Define a Community for Progressive Ideas.** The first step is to determine the identity of the members of the philanthropic community who will participate in the philanthropic covenant. Are we speaking of large foundations and community foundations? Does the community include smaller foundations, individual philanthropists, and giving circles? What about corporations and governmental officials and policy makers?

- **Step Two: Convene the Community.** Build the bonds. Do the members of the community have shared values? Is civic engagement fundamental to philanthropy in their view? We suggest the community-building technique called "story sharing," in which a trained facilitator leads participants to share their experiences with each other. The subject matter of the circle would be to share our unique experiences with philanthropy: what projects work; what projects don't work, and why. We would seek to understand the extent to which citizen participation may influence a project's success.

- **Step Three: Reconvene the Community.** Trust, affirmation, mutual understanding, and deep commitment are necessary ingredients to the success of this community-building exercise. Therefore, the story sharing and convening should be repeated at least twice before any agenda-setting is attempted.

- **Step Four: Agree on Process.** The community must agree on a process for setting priorities.

- **Step Five: Action.** The community is finally ready to define an action plan and funding strategy to make real their progressive agenda and ideas. The plan would likely include an analysis to lead to more strategic grantmaking in the progressive ideas sector; a funding strategy for grassroots philanthropy; and a funding strategy for civic engagement/ democratic practice. The plan would also include a coordinated support strategy that would train the next generation of progressive thinkers and activists; build an infrastructure of think tanks and advocacy groups; invest in media and media transparency; fund legal organizations; support religious organizations; and create working networks of philanthropic institutions.

What the Community Organizations and Local Faith Communities Can Do

Many individuals and organizations within and outside our community are already working very hard on each of the Covenant-agenda items. The overall purpose of this good work is to make life better for our communities. Many of these organizations are woefully under-resourced—both in terms of cash and human resources. As organizations seek to increase the effectiveness of their efforts, the challenge is often grounded in resources, and the harsh reality is that if such organizations do not greatly multiply and increase their financial and human resources, they will fail. Here are some steps that community organizations, including faith-based organizations, can take to increase their effectiveness in this regard:

- Recognize the importance of strategic planning and capacity building. Raise funds specifically for this effort as you solicit donations and seek funding.
- Register your organization with Volunteer Match: www.volunteermatch.org.
- Write and implement a fundraising strategy.

What Every Individual Can Do Now

Former president Bill Clinton's latest book, entitled *Giving*, provides an excellent framework around which individual citizens can have in impact in philanthropy. These strategies demonstrate that every gift matters, and that you don't have to give a Buffett-sized gift to make a difference.

- **Read *Giving*.** Pay special attention to the stories collected about everyday citizens and the difference that they have made in the world. These stories are inspiring, and as we read about the actions of others, we are better able to imagine our own capacity for real change.
- **Give Money.**
  - You do not have to be a billionaire. Your giving should be proportional to your income. Tithing is one of the oldest traditions in black America. Try to set aside at least 10 percent of your income for charity. If you cannot handle 10 percent, pick another percentage, and stick to it. One of the stories Clinton tells in his book is about two Minnesota sixth graders who set a goal of collecting only $1 from each of their peers to contribute to Katrina relief. When all was said and done, their modest goal-setting turned into a $24,000 gift to the victims of the hurricane.[48]
  - Join or form a giving circle. A giving circle is a group of donors who place their charitable dollars into a pooled fund, and decide as a group which charities to support. They can vary in size, structure, and charitable focus. Giving circles have exploded as an innovative way that ordinary Americans can have an enormous impact in philanthropy. A recent study estimates that giving circles have raised about $88 million since 2000 and show no signs of slowing down.[49] The 10 basic steps to forming a giving circle are available on the website of the Forum of Regional Associations of Grantmakers at www.givingforum.org.[50]

- Encourage others to give. Network with your family and friends. Let them know about the organizations and ideas that you find interesting and important. Remind them of their moral obligation to give back to their religious institution, community organization, or school. Black colleges have endowments and alumni giving rates that are among the lowest in the nation.[51]

- **Give Time.** While we may not all have access to money, everyone has access to 168 hours each and every week. Sometimes the gift of time can be more rewarding and long-lasting than money. Visit www.VolunteerMatch.org to locate volunteer organizations near you. Volunteer opportunities include mentoring, tutoring, lending professional skills, home-building, life-skills/financial skills coaching, and even story sharing. In his book, President Clinton recounts the volunteer work of a 22-year old young woman in Lesotho, Africa, and the impact she was having on hundreds, simply by sharing her story.[52] Volunteerism is one of the most important indicators of civic health and participation in a democracy. Though people so often equate civic participation with merely voting or monetary contributions, our democracy simply could not thrive without *volunteerism*.

- **Give Things.** Most Americans are blessed with an overabundance of things that we use to make our everyday lives more convenient. Individuals seeking to make a difference, and who want to give more than just money should also consider donating useful items. The challenge is, of course, to donate items that are truly useful to people in need, rather than items of little or no value. *Giving* sets forth stories about several organizations that specialize in making this assessment. Doc to Dock is an organization that collects and delivers medical supplies and pharmaceuticals to health

111

providers in Africa and the Middle East.[53] The U.S.–Africa Children's Fellowship collects and donates educational materials, school supplies, toys, and games and donates them to the Zimbabwe Organization of Rural Associations for Progress.[54] Other useful items that can be collected and donated are bicycles, cars, furniture, construction supplies, musical instruments, and sports equipment. Items can even be auctioned on eBay with the proceeds going to charity.

- **Give Skills.** One of the most useful things that someone can give is a special skill. Skills in demand include: tutoring, life-skills coaching, financial skills coaching, and professionals skills such as lawyering or health care. Diverse professionals such as hair stylists, cosmetologists, engineers, social workers, and psychologists can find a great demand for their skills depending on the particular situation. Be creative. Keep an open mind. And search out or create opportunities to volunteer whenever they arise.

What Works Now

The W.K. Kellogg Foundation: Providing Resources to Make Civic Engagement a Priority and a Reality

The W.K. Kellogg Foundation (WKKF) provides a model for large, established foundations to cultivate change through philanthropy and volunteerism. First, it recognizes that civic engagement should be a central component of all movements for social change. This recognition, while seemingly obvious, represents the kind of prioritizing necessary to create the change this chapter advocates.

The WKKF has created a framework for increasing civic engagement with three strategies for increasing the engagement of citizens in democracy: supporting emerging leaders and donors, creating and sharing knowledge, and building tools for nonprofit sustainability and innovative giving. Such goals are not simply lofty rhetoric for WKKF; it does not merely dole out money. Instead, the foundation seeks to invest time and resources into organizations that can advance their goal of effecting social change, building lasting relationships that lead to more effective use of funds. Examples of WKKF's investment in civic engagement include the following:

- The Dorothy A. Johnson Center for Philanthropy and Non-Profit Leadership, which conducts research on effective strategies for foundations and nonprofit organizations and shares that research for the benefit of all.
- The National Service-Learning Partnership, a national network of members dedicated to advancing service-learning as a core part of every young person's education. The Partnership concentrates on strengthening the impact of service-learning on young people's learning and development, especially their academic and civic preparation.
- The Youth Innovation Fund, a program implemented at eight sites nationwide that seeks to empower young people to study local problems and implement local solutions, in an effort to both improve communities and teach youth about their own power to effect change.

Additionally, WKKF joins grant recipients into cohorts to encourage the sharing of innovative ideas, best practices, and common objectives so that smaller organizations can achieve maximum impact. One such cohort, joining leaders of organizations seeking to increase civic engagement, provides a real model for the philanthropic community generally and more specifically the black philanthropic community. Leaders will participate in a retreat to share knowledge and devise effective strategies. This sharing and learning is crucial to the movement of the philanthropic covenant, to maximize effectiveness by working together toward shared goals.

Democracy Alliance: Strategic Investments in Organizations as Agents of Change

The Democracy Alliance provides a model for strategic philanthropy to increase progressive ideas and induce action. First, it seeks out organizations known as "capacity builders," groups that produce new ideas, develop new technologies, and mobilize people to continue their work. Secondly, Democracy Alliance provides a variety of funding based on the specific need of the recipient organization, referred to as the Partner. This financial assistance can include seed capital, growth capital, and funding to increase management capacity. By providing targeted financial assistance, they can maximize the short-term impact and long-term sustainability of Partner organizations. Additionally, this financial assistance is coupled with strategic collaboration, as Democracy Alliance seeks to create a portfolio of groups that will work together to create strategic alliances and therefore maximum impact.

Recipients of Democracy Alliance's investments include the following:

- The Center for Progressive Leadership, an organization that trains diverse, progressive leaders to make an impact and create social change in a variety of political arenas, including political office, private sector, and grassroots activism.

- Women's Voices, Women's Votes, a group seeking to include unmarried women in the political process through voting and advocacy. The organization not only seeks to increase voting among this demographic, but also to mobilize these women to "turnkey," or pass on, their new knowledge and expand the movement further.

Oprah Winfrey: Inspiring Giving and Engagement by Individual Philanthropy

Oprah Winfrey provides a model of black philanthropy on two levels. Individually, she has donated huge amounts of money to needy causes. In 2004, she became the first black philanthropist to make the *BusinessWeek* magazine "Top 50 Most Generous Philanthropists," donating an estimated $175 million up to that time. Figures today estimate that Oprah has increased her individual philanthropy, giving over $58 million in 2006 alone. Recipients of her aid include projects designed to increase civic engagement, including the following:

- O Ambassadors, a new program seeking to join 1000 schools across the United States and Canada as partners in creating school-based clubs that teach children about global issues and help them raise funds to address problems such as poverty, hunger, and limited access to education. The program seeks "to inspire young people to become active, compassionate and knowledgeable global citizens."[55]
- Oprah's Angel Network, which has constructed over 60 schools in 13 countries and engaged in countless domestic projects, such as teaming with Habitat for Humanity to build 900 homes in areas affected by Hurricanes Katrina and Rita.

A Philanthropic Covenant with Black America

However, Oprah's generosity and impact on the philanthropic community is not limited to her own donations. Perhaps her more lasting legacy will be her work to empower everyday citizens to give back, through donations, volunteering, and increased awareness of pressing social issues. Oprah has used her unique position and visibility to start the Angel Network, which seeks to make the show's viewers partners in Oprah's good works. Her website includes a variety of resources for getting involved, from a searchable database of worthy organizations to an entire section devoted to helping individuals figure out how to give within their means. It also features a section on making your gift effective, echoing the goals of strategic philanthropy advocated by this article.

Her latest venture takes philanthropy to new levels. A new reality show entitled, *The Big Give*, premiered in March 2008. On the show, contestants will compete to come up with creative ways to use money and resources provided by Oprah to multiply their funds before giving the earnings away to charity. The model is similar to a past Oprah show, where the host gave the audience $1,000 each that had to be used to benefit a worthy cause. By making giving fun, Oprah seeks to launch philanthropy into popular culture, continuing her theme of empowering citizens to make change through individual giving.

Fundamentally, Oprah has provided inspiration, a model of a successful black woman who takes great pride in generosity and helps ordinary citizens to do the same. She teaches people to achieve the change they seek through targeted philanthropy, possible for people of all income levels. Her mission statement in starting the Angel Network in 1997 says it best, "[I wanted to] inspire people to use their lives and to reap the truest rewards that come from giving to others."

Notes

1. Justice Louis D. Brandeis.

2. Alexander De Tocqueville, *Democracy in America*, ed. J.P. Mayer (New York: Harper Collins Publishers, 1966).

3. Ibid.

4. John Bridgeland, "Philanthropy's Role in a Civic Awakening" (May 2005), available at www.pacefunders.org/essays.html, p. 2.

5. Ibid.

6. See William Schambra, "Problem of Philanthropy for Civic Renewal," PACE (May 2005) available at www.pacefunders.org/pdf/essays.

7. Ibid.

8. Ibid., at 2.

9. See William A. Schambra, "The Ungodly Bright: Should they Lead Philanthropy Into The Future?" In *Giving Well, Doing Good: Readings for Thoughtful Philanthropists*, ed. Amy Kass (Bloomington: Indiana University Press, 2008), pp. 471–478.

10. Schambra, "Problem of Philanthropy for Civic Renewal," p. 3.

11. See, e.g., The Open Society Institute, the Rockefeller Brothers Fund, the W.K. Kellogg Foundation, the Ford Foundation, and the Carnegie Corporation.

12. Bridgeland, "Philanthropy's Role," pp. 3–7. Bridgeland's recommendations included such suggestions as supporting the establishment of civic indicators, creating a fund to support innovative and results-oriented initiatives, and supporting dialogues on how to strengthen civic philanthropy.

13. The Strategic Philanthropy of Conservative Foundations, available at http://www.mediatransparency.org/conservativephilanthropy.php.

14. Ibid.

15. See Robert M. Franklin, *Crisis in the Village: Restoring Hope in African American Communities* (Minneapolis: Augsbury Fortress Press, 2007), p. 236.

16. Bridgeland, "Philanthropy's Role," p. 3.

17. Marybeth Gasman, "New Trends in African American Philanthropy," *Observations on Philanthropy*, March 3, 2006, p. 1.

18. Ibid.

19. See generally Franklin, *Crisis in the Village*, pp. 217–243.

20. Enola G. Aird, Lorraine Blackman, Obie Clayton, Stephanie Robinson, *Our Foundational Covenant*, (Cambridge, MA: Jamestown Project Press, 2007), p. 9. Available at www.jamestownproject.org.

21. Michelle Nunn, "Reinvigorating Democratic Participation and Activating an Engaged Citizenry" (May 2005), available at www.pacefunders.org/essays.html.

22. Ibid.

23. Ibid.

24. Ibid.

25. Brian Faler, "Election Turnout was Highest since 1968," *Washington Post*, January 15, 2005, available at www.washingtonpost.com.

26. Bureau of Labor Statistics, "Volunteering in the United States, 2006" (September 2006), available at www.bls.gov/news.release/volun.toc.htm.

27. Thomas H. Sander and Robert D. Putnam, "Sept. 11 as Civics Lesson," *Washington Post*, September 10, 2005, available at www.washingtonpost.com.

28. Media Transparency and Cursor, Inc., "The Strategic Philanthropy of Conservative Foundations: Moving a Public Policy Agenda," available at http://www.mediatransparency.org/conservativephilanthropy.php.

29. Ibid.

30. Ibid.

31. Carolyn M. Brown: "America's leading black philanthropists: giving back is one of the major tenets of the Black Enterprise Declaration of Financial Empowerment. In doing so, we advocate using money to develop our community and build wealth. On the following pages meet America's largest, and most strategic, black philanthropists," *Black Enterprise*, August 2005. Quoting from the report of New Ventures in Philanthropy, available at www.givingforum.org.

32. Bridgeland, "Philanthropy's Role."

33. Michael Anft and Harvey Lipman, "How Americans Give," *Chronicle on Philanthropy*, May 1, 2003.

34. Gasman, "New Trends in African American Philanthropy."

35. Ibid.

36. Ibid.

37. Felina Mottino and Eugene Miller, "Pathways for Change: Philanthropy Among African American, Asian American and Latino Donors in the New York Metropolitan Region." Center on Philanthropy and Civil Society in partnership with the Coalition for New Philanthropy, 2005.

38. Ibid.

39. Ibid.

40. Ibid.

41. Ibid.

42. Bureau of Labor Statistics, "Volunteering in the United States, 2006" (September 2006), available at www.bls.gov/news.release/volun.toc.htm.

43. National Association for the Advancement of Colored People, "Civic Engagement," available at http://www.naacp.org/advocacy/civic/.

44. Ibid.

45. Mark Hugo Lopez, "Electoral Engagement among Minority Youth," Fact Sheet of The Center for Information and Research on Civic Learning and Engagement" (July 2005).

46. Lonnie R. Sherrod, "Promoting the Development of Citizenship in Diverse Youth," available online at www.apsanet.org, April 2003. For a further discussion of African-American youth engagement, see: Cathy Cohen's "African American Youth: Broadening our Understanding of Politics, Civic Engagement and Activism" (June 2006), available at www.ssrc.org.

47. Center for Information & Research on Civic Learning & Engagement, "2006 Civic and Political Health of the Nation Survey," available at http://www.civicyouth.org/research/products/youth_index.htm.

48. Bill Clinton, *Giving* (New York: Knopf, 2007), p. 28.

49. Elizabeth Schwinn, "Donor 'Giving Circles' Awarded $13-Million in Grants Last Year," *Chronicle of Philanthropy*, May 18, 2007, available at http://philanthropy.com/free/update/2007/05/2007051802.htm.

50. "Ten Basic Steps to Starting a Giving Circle," available at http://www.givingforum.org/s_forum/doc.asp?CID=1832&DID=5108.

51. Marybeth Gasman and Noah D. Drezner, "Payback Time: Katrina and the Nation's Obligation to Black Colleges," *onPhilanthropy*, February 3, 2006, available at www.onphilanthropy.com/site/News2?page=NewsArticle&id=5696.

52. Clinton, *Giving,* pp. 42–43.

53. Clinton, *Giving,* pp. 56–57.

54. Clinton, *Giving,* p. 58.

55. Oprah's Angel Network, "O Ambassadors," available at http://www.oambassadors.org/global/about-the-program.

Chapter 6

An African American Response to Natural Disasters

Reflecting on Hurricanes Katrina and Rita

Sherece Y. West, Ph.D.
Former CEO, Louisiana Disaster Recovery Foundation,
Baton Rouge, LA

Kermit "K.C." Burton
Former loaned executive, Louisiana Disaster Recovery Foundation,
Baton Rouge, LA

One would logically conclude that a natural disaster would be an equalizer. Emotionally and financially, all people who are victims of a natural disaster experience trauma and loss. Homes, neighborhoods, even entire communities are damaged or destroyed. There is loss of life, loss of community, loss of stability.

A Philanthropic Covenant with Black America

Regardless of one's race and economic status, it would appear that Hurricanes Katrina and Rita impacted all communities the same way. That is what has been reported by the media, government, and those communities with voice (primarily white and more affluent communities). According to Jed Horne, author of *Breach of Faith* and editor of the *Times-Picayune*, "Rich people died along with the indigent. The pricy homes of the professional class, both black and white, were destroyed, as were rickety cottages owned or rented by the poor. That did not make Katrina an 'equal opportunity destroyer,' as some hastened to call it. Poor blacks did disproportionately more of the dying. And as the engines of recovery creaked into gear, people of means enjoyed advantages that had been theirs all along."

The statistics are too familiar; not a year goes by without a hurricane, tornado, flood, or drought adversely impacting the South. Because of its simple geological and meteorological placement, it is a plain fact that this region is more vulnerable to natural disasters. Unfortunately, what is also a plain fact is that when disasters strike, African Americans are often disproportionately without resources to respond and recover. This fact basically creates a breach between government and the black communities of the South. With Katrina, not only were the levees breached, but the responsibility of the federal and state governments to provide equal disaster recovery to African American citizens was also breeched. From Jim Crow to the present, these black communities are "racialized," a term coined by Harvard Law Professor Lani Guanier, author of *The Miner's Canary*. African Americans of the South are part of racialized communities. These communities are excluded from a democratic social community and fail to receive the full protections and benefits of government. These communities experience structural racism that marginalizes them while extending privileges to white society.

Race, particularly in the South, is like the miner's canary. Miners, as a past practice, often carried a canary into the mine alongside them. The canary's more fragile respiratory system would cause it to collapse from noxious gases long before humans were affected, thus alerting the miners to danger. The canary's distress signaled that there was poison in the air. Racially marginalized black communities of the South are like the miner's canary. Their distress is the first sign of the eminent danger of racism. When we discuss Hurricanes Katrina, Rita, or even Gustav or Ike, we fail to address racism. We inquire about the physical conditions of the levees—where were they breached?— but we don't fully address the social and economic conditions of black communities that result from such breaches. Nor do we ask whether these communities were breached by the government as well. If government, in fact, breached its obligations to black communities in the face of natural disasters, then we also need to ask: What covenants can be reached between the black community and government to address racism and advance pluralism? And what roles can the public and private sectors play in that process. (Webster's dictionary defines *breach* as a violation of a law, obligation, or promise. It defines *covenant* as a binding obligation, promise, or pledge.)

Presently, Congress is mulling over legislation to provide federal recovery support in the aftermath of Hurricanes Gustav and Ike. Former Presidents George H. W. Bush and Bill Clinton have teamed up to form the Bush Clinton Coastal Recovery Fund to address relief for communities ravaged by Gustav and Ike.

How might African American leaders, black institutions, and black community social capital efforts be organized to repair the breach and prevent any future breaches? How will these leaders, institutions, and communities prepare for future hurricanes and other natural disasters? What covenants will be reached between the black community and the public and private sectors? And, finally, what type of covenant or accord will be reached between the black community and philanthropy?

This chapter addresses disaster recovery and preparedness through the lens of the African American community. It also mentions some viable ways organized philanthropy has supported and how philanthropy, in general, can heighten its support of the black community.

In the late 1990s with the W. K. Kellogg Foundation's "Repairing the Breach" Initiative, African American leaders discussed at length how to support family life, reclaim communities, and rebuild civic society in America's communities. A task force chaired by former Atlanta Mayor and U.N. Ambassador Andrew Young probed into how the government, especially the federal government, could repair the breach caused by decades of broken promises and pledges made to address poverty and disenfranchisement in the black community. The South was identified as the region with the least amount of progress made toward tackling these marginalized communities.

As advocates, African American leaders must be a voice for their communities in advocating for government policies and practices that outline the responsibilities of government to address disaster-impacted communities with enough funding and relief service supports to get the job done. Local leaders must be prepared to hold all tiers of government—federal, state, county, and municipal—accountable for doing their duties and meeting their responsibilities in times of disaster.

As leaders, they must be reliable and close to the ground to provide timely problem solving and decision making in cooperation with elected and appointed government officials. These leaders must be prepared to work with government to bring together a variety of stakeholders including business, organized labor, universities, hospitals, and others. They must work together, utilizing nonjurisdictional power, to reach a consensus and resolve conflicts through compromise and trust building. They must also gather ideas generated by the black community and relay them to government, media, and the public. And, above all, these leaders must strive to build and support community institutions.

Preparing Before the Breaches: Readiness and Response and the Role of Black Institutions

A recent publication entitled *Power Amidst Chaos* authored by the Alliance for Justice (in partnership with the Louisiana Disaster Recovery Foundation and the Foundation for the Mid-South) addresses "vulnerability before the breaches." Prior to Katrina and Rita, there was a serious lack of a practical and well-communicated disaster-preparedness strategies or evacuation planning. Black institutions, particularly black churches, historically black colleges and universities and other "anchored institutions," can play an important role in addressing readiness and rapid response.

Faith-based organizations have demonstrated the ability (with Katrina and Rita) to act as frontline responders to quickly mobilize their congregations to provide food, shelter, and relief. Black churches have been highly successful in amassing a significant level of relief funds and placing families with other out-of-state congregations.

Historically black colleges and universities have proven instrumental in providing ad hoc infrastructure and facilities to house and care for people impacted by the hurricanes. Hospitals affiliated with these universities were prepared to provide emergency and ongoing medical care. Colleges and universities furnished thousands of student volunteers to help with response and relief efforts.

These churches, universities, and hospitals are highly recognizable institutions in the black community. According to Arabella Philanthropic Advisors in its publication, *Investing in Disaster Response*, there are some common obstacles that prevent readiness and rapid response. There are many low-visibility disaster response organizations that the public knows little about. There are also increasing concerns from the public about credibility and trust related to a number of relief organizations. And slow disaster relief and response have been blamed for the inability to reach the most at-risk communities. Black anchored institutions allay many of these fears and apprehensions in the black community. They are a known and trusted quantity.

Promoting the Covenants: Empowerment and Engagement and the Role of Black Social Capital

African American leaders and black institutions are not sufficient, by themselves, to better prepare black communities for natural and other disasters. Specific work within black communities is also required, and the black community must lead it. As early twentieth-century New York journalist Don Marquis remarked, "When a man tells you he got rich through hard work, ask him: 'whose?'" Black communities working to change black communities are what will make the policy gains meaningful. Perhaps Oprah Winfrey, media star and noted philanthropist, expresses it best in saying, "Unless you do great things with it, it makes no difference how much you are rewarded, or how much power you have." A number of leaders believe great things will result from developing disaster-related covenants.

There is a wealth of social capital in the black community. In his book, *Better Together: Restoring the Community*, Harvard Professor Robert D. Putnam defines social capital as "elements of social networks, norms of reciprocity, mutual assistance, and trustworthiness alive in a local community." The black community is rich with social capital through families, churches, neighborhood businesses, and civic associations.

The challenge to the black community is how to mobilize this capital to form covenants with the public and private sectors to ensure that these local communities reach a level of well-being on a par with more affluent communities. Better schools and hospitals, more banking, shopping, transportation and job options, and improved relations with law enforcement, the courts, and the media are among the core elements needed for a healthy community. The relative health of a community represents a major factor in how it can prepare and respond to a hurricane, flood, or blackout. For a healthier black community, core covenants need to be reached with various public and private sector partners.

Social capital has the kinetic potential to inspire commitment and action. It has the ability to build broad-based involvement of families, churches, local businesses, and civic groups. Social capital fosters hope and participation through its grassroots networks. It has all the local ingredients to promote sustainable covenants.

Family, public-, and private-sector covenants along with covenants with the nonprofit sector and within black communities for community-wide preparation will make policy and other structural changes actionable and sustainable. They will benefit the community by ensuring disaster preparation, protection, preservation of community culture, and equitable and inclusive disaster-related performance by all parties. Framed by the 10 covenants of *The Covenant with Black America*—health care and well-being; public education potential and achievement; correcting unequal justice; community-centered policing; access to affordable neighborhoods connected to opportunity; claiming democracy; strengthening rural roots; accessing jobs, wealth and prosperity; ensuring environmental justice; and closing the racial digital divide—we believe there are additional, finite or embedded covenants for black community disaster readiness and responsiveness.

Among them, for example, the black community must make specific covenants for change with a variety of sectors: health, banking and finance, legal, educational, media (including information and entertainment media), as well as personal and family support networks. A separate treatise could be written about each of these, but there is one need they all, with the exception of the media, share in common: the need for important personal, financial, business and organizational records to be up-to-date and backed-up somewhere outside the disaster prone area.

Inadequate or destroyed records remain problematic for many black individual and family victims of Hurricanes Katrina and Rita more than two years after the storms struck the Gulf Coast. Loss of such records constitutes a significant barrier to resolving legal and financial issues relating to property and insurance matters, delays school enrollment and health care, and much more.

Additionally, covenants with the health sector could, among many things, focus upon assuring physical check-ups and records check-ups for all black citizens within 12 months of their last birthday and annually thereafter. A covenant with the banking and finance sector could be for every black household to have at least one formal checking, savings, and investment connection to at least one nonpredatory and otherwise reputable financial institution. The legal sector could covenant with the black community for every black adult over a specific age (such as 25 years old) to have a will written and legally filed.

Media might covenant around making nonprofits and faith institutions that serve black communities better known and better supported in and out of times of crisis and disaster. Schools and education centers can covenant to become community centers for convening and learning, as well as potential storage places for brooms, shovels, tools, and other basic recovery supplies and equipment. And black families, their neighbors, friends, family support, and social networks must covenant to plan for emergencies and disasters so everyone has someone to track and common places for checking in and tracking; and so food, transportation, medicines and other essentials, and culturally or historically important items are readied for preservation or use should emergency or disaster strike.

There should similarly be covenants specifically within black communities for community-wide preparation. Evacuees who've returned to New Orleans for the post-Katrina recovery sometimes realize best how important it is to better prepare black communities. Often their experiences help them have more urgency than ever before about changing things that make black communities disproportionately vulnerable. As Nelson Mandela remarked in his book, *A Long Walk to Freedom*, "There is nothing like returning to a place that remains unchanged to find ways in which you yourself have [been] altered." Covenants within black communities for progress should adhere to and demand respect and consideration for traditional African American rights and values.

Equally as important, intracommunity efforts should include creating strategies for pooling human and financial capital, and fully and strategically using organizing and political strengths.

Another way the disproportionate disadvantage experienced by black communities is evidenced is with the overdevelopment of big box stores, major grocery chains, corporate office, and warehouse centers. Instead, there is the dire need to redevelop hospitals, universities, schools, and other institutional anchors; as well as community-based and community-centered nonprofit institutions.

While the sector is welcomed and should be thanked more often for the necessary services they provide, the sector nonetheless should be held more accountable by the black community for having cultural competency and efficiency, for collaborative advocacy, and for producing results that assist in reducing the very need for their services. Especially for disaster situations, there should be a covenant with the nonprofit sector for accountability, triaging, and coordinating services; allocating support to and from individuals, families, communities, organizations, houses of worship, and other faith-related centers; and for creating networks among black community-serving nonprofits to ensure better communication and service, especially in disaster, crisis, and emergency situations.

Supporting the Covenants: Revitalization and Transformation and the Role of Philanthropy

Further, a covenant between blacks and the nonprofit sector should exist around better engaging and guiding philanthropic efforts for black communities, especially with regard to disaster readiness and responsiveness. As important as large grants and charity continue to be to the relief and recovery needs of

Hurricane Katrina and Rita affected areas, for black communities, simply giving money from the philanthropic sector has not proven to be enough. The philanthropic sector has more than money: attributes of knowledge, connections, convening ability, influence, leveragability and so forth that should be covenanted with the black community for provision, especially in disaster situations. "The excellence of a gift," wrote Charles Dudley Warner in *Eleventh Study*, "lies in its appropriateness rather than in its value."

For organized philanthropy, funding should be more intentional and focus on investing in advocacy, supporting grassroots leadership, providing flexible funding for infrastructure improvements for preparedness and rapid response, building the capacity of anchored institutions, and fostering sustainability for social capital networks.

With a new president, his Administration should re-establish the White House Interagency Task Force on Nonprofits and Government. During the Clinton Administration, the Council on Foundations collaborated with the federal government to make strategic investments in marginalized communities across the nation. The Clinton Administration built "partnerships for a stronger civil society." One partnership that stands out was funding provided to the Southern Institute on Children & Families to address health care for uninsured children and regional efforts to promote child care.

This partnership received funding from the Robert Wood Johnson Foundation and the David and Lucile Packard Foundation.

For certain, it is important to become more strategic about linking philanthropy and black communities for the betterment of these communities and to enhance synergies with other communities. The philanthropic sector, including philanthropy by the black community itself, is a keystone in improving the readiness, responsiveness, and rebuilding from emergencies and disasters. The black community must covenant to make philanthropy a better understood component of "community," and not simply a source of dollars.

Zora Neale Hurston wrote in *Dust Tracks On a Road*, "Mama exhorted her children at every opportunity to 'jump at de sun.' We might not land on de sun but at least we would get off de ground." Covenants are at least steps in a good direction. And as Marion Wright Edelman, founder and CEO of the Children's Defense Fund, said, "We must not, in trying to think about how we can make a big difference, ignore the small differences we can make which, over time, add up to big differences that we often cannot foresee."

There are small steps the black community can covenant to take as a community that can institutionalize diverse philanthropic engagement in ongoing strengthening and broad value for blacks and their communities. Leaders should covenant to encourage legacy philanthropy in communities. African Americans die leaving too much wealth in forms that neither benefit families or their communities.

A Black Philanthropic Covenant should include a commitment of support for wealth-building strategies. Blacks should covenant with the philanthropic sector overall to support black funds, especially to create disaster/crisis-related strategies and pools of ready liquid assets. Such funds, as at the Twenty-First Century Foundation (21CF) and Faith Partnerships Inc., provided important resources after Hurricane Katrina, and 21CF has afforded that organization an ongoing convening power and credibility in the post-Katrina Gulf Coast.

The black community should covenant with the philanthropic sector and other public and private funders to support better education for the public regarding disaster/crisis readiness and response for black communities, including how predisaster structural realities increase disaster/crisis vulnerabilities for many black communities. Three other things black communities should covenant include (1) supporting improved organization of philanthropy by faith-based organizations and their related organizations; (2) engaging high net worth black individuals to invest around issues of black community disaster, crisis readiness and responsiveness; and (3) regularly convening the black philanthropic sector about the same thing. Black communities contribute to sustained vulnerability if it depends too heavily upon external philanthropy and resources. As Oprah Winfrey said about overcoming her personal history of struggle and disaster, "I chose to rise up out of that storm and see that in moments of desperation, fear and hopelessness, each of us can be a rainbow of hope—doing what we can to extend ourselves in kindness and grace to one another. And I know for sure that there are no them . . . there's only us."

The black community must covenant with others but do its part for itself, too. In or out of disaster, this should be its most important covenant to actualize.

Forty-five years ago, Dr. Martin Luther King, Jr. wrote from a Birmingham jail:

> *I have traveled the length and breadth of Alabama, Mississippi and all the other southern states. On sweltering summer days and crisp autumn mornings. I have looked at the South's beautiful churches with their lofty spires pointing heavenly. I have beheld the impressive outlines of massive education buildings.*

These churches and universities must stand strong with black leaders to help communities weather the storms. Philanthropy can help to buttress a strong framework for the future. The black community must remain resolved and make covenants sustainable and ready to withstand any type of breach—by levees, government, or any breach of faith.

The Equity and Inclusion Campaign

The Equity & Inclusion Campaign, an initiative of the Louisiana Disaster Recovery Foundation (LDRF), is a public policy and public messaging campaign advocating for fulfillment of the federal commitment to confront persistent poverty and equity during the Gulf Coast recovery. The campaign draws together leaders from three hurricane-affected states—Louisiana, Mississippi, and Alabama—to combine their voices and coordinate their efforts to advocate for "more equitable and inclusionary government policies." African Americans from ACORN, Alabama Arise, Churches Supporting Churches, Louisiana Justice Institute, and Mississippi NAACP are among the most prominent leaders of the Campaign.

The Japan Foundation

The Center for Global Partnership, an initiative of The Japan Foundation, developed an exchange project between Kobe and New Orleans: the Japan Interaction Project for Cooperation for Hurricane Katrina Recovery & Reconstruction. Leaders from both Kobe and New Orleans met with one another in a series of meetings in Japan and Louisiana. Among the Louisiana delegation were prominent black local leaders, including Oliver Thomas, former president of the New Orleans City Council; Joseph R. Matthews, director of the New Orleans Office of Emergency Preparedness; and Vera Billy Triplett, assistant professor at Our Lady of Holy Cross College. While in New Orleans, the Japanese delegation visited and met with a number of black faith-based organizations and academicians at Xavier University.

In Japan, academic and elected leaders shared their disaster preparedness and response plans during visits and meetings at Kyoto University and Meiji University.

There is an ongoing dialogue between Kobe and New Orleans and plans to continue to share mutual best practices and lessons learned.

The Twenty-First Century Foundation

The Hurricane Katrina Recovery Fund is a program of the Twenty-First Century Foundation. The fund provides support to invest in African American leaders and black institutions to help to rebuild the lives of black people and their respective communities impacted by the storms. The fund provides support to faith-based and other community-based organizations to help them re-establish themselves within their respective neighborhoods. It also provides support for efforts to build the capacity of these organizations to prepare and respond to future disasters. A core aspect of its funding supports local community organizing.

The New York Regional Associations of Grantmakers

The Gulf Coast Recovery Task Force, a special initiative of the New York Regional Association of Grantmakers (NYRAG), is comprised of 50-plus members representing private, public, and corporate organized philanthropy. Since 2005, the NYRAG Task Force has collaborated with 90-plus sister foundations of the Greater New York Tri-State area to provide funding to 950 nonprofit organizations in 196 communities in the Gulf Coast states and across 35 other states (those outside groups providing recovery and relief services) and four countries.

The Task Force offers some advice from its publication *Best Practices in Disaster Grantmaking* that can offer some food for thought for a Black Philanthropic Covenant. Among some recommendations: utilize key people in the affected communities; utilize existing relationships to gather information; be willing to take risks; share information with other funders and nonprofits; create a dynamic funder collaborative; create a nationally relevant information resource; put staff on the ground; be proactive; create collaborative funding efforts; strengthen local philanthropy; defer a portion of grant dispersal; expand funding focus; and simplify the application process.

References

Davidson, Oliver, and Margaret Siegel. 2006. *Investing in disaster response.* Arabella Philanthropic Investment Brief.

Fabrizio, Ray, Edith Karas, and Ruth Menmuir. 1970. *The rhetoric of no.* New York: Holt, Rinehart & Winston.

Gardner, John W. 1990. *On leadership.* New York: Macmillan Publishing.

Guanier, Lani, and Gerald Torres. 2002. *The miner's canary: Enlisting race, resisting power, transforming democracy.* Cambridge: Harvard University Press.

Horne, Jed. 2006. *Breach of faith: Hurricane Katrina and the near death of a great American city.* New York: Random House.

Hurston, Zora Neale. 1996. *Dust tracks on a road.* New York: Harper Perennial.

Interagency Task Force on Nonprofits & Government. 2000. *Partnerships for a stronger civil society* (a Report to President William J. Clinton). Washington, DC: Government Printing Office, December.

King, Martin Luther, Jr. 1963. *Why we can't wait.* New York: Harper & Row.

Mandela, Nelson. 2006. *Long walk to freedom*. Boston: Little, Brown Press.

New York Regional Association of Grantmakers. 2007. *Best practices in disaster grantmaking*. New York: NYRAG Publication.

Putnam, Robert D., and Lewis M. Feldstein. 2003. *Better together: Restoring the American community*. New York: Simon & Schuster.

Sagawa, Shirley, and Eli Segal. 2000. *Common interest common good: Creating value through business and social sector partnerships*. Cambridge: Harvard University Press.

Taida, Hideya. 2006. *From Kobe to New Orleans: Lessons learned from the great Hanshin-Awaji earthquake. From New Orleans to Tokyo: Lessons from Hurricane Katrina*. Japan Foundation Press.

Usdin, Linda. 2007. *Power amidst chaos: Foundation support for advocacy related to disasters*. Alliance for Justice Press.

Chapter 7

Families and Friends—The Power of Small Groups

Carol Brunson Day

CEO, National Black Child Development Institute, Washington, DC

Judith Gordon Samuel

Partner, Samuel Consulting LLC, Chicago, IL

T his chapter describes outstanding models already in place
in the black community for mobilizing small groups of
people to consolidate and focus their resources on improving themselves and their community. Two such examples
are families who organize reunions and giving circles. We will
explore both of these examples by sharing two case studies:
one reflects a family that has maintained its ties to the land be-
queathed to ancestors in 1850; and the other case study examines
the experience of a group of young women who sought to give

back to the black community over a 30-year period. We will conclude this chapter with an analysis of the commonalities between giving circles and family reunions and their ability to build and sustain wealth within black communities, strengthen black families, and encourage others, particularly future generations, to do the same.

African American Family Reunions

According to *Ebony* magazine in April 2002, "there were over 200,000 family reunions each year in the United States, with about 8 million people attending them each year."

The uniting of family members from different regions and generations is evident in many countries and ethnic groups. However, in the United States, media attention seems to focus on African American family reunions. Perhaps this is due to the popularity of Alex Haley's book, *Roots,* which inspired many African Americans to research their past and share this information with their extended families at reunions.

Research by Ione D. Vargus, Chair of the Family Reunion Institute of Temple University, suggests that the tradition of African American reunions began with the African tradition of "family" as the center of the religious, economic, and political unit. When this "family unit" was disrupted by slavery, African Americans went about putting the family back together after slavery was abolished. Former slaves tried to reconnect with their families and continued to care for and raise the children and kin of other families as they had done during slavery.[1] The aunts, uncles, grandparents and unrelated individuals became part of the "extended family" who were honored, recognized, reconnected and "loved" at family gatherings.

140

African American family reunions began as one-day picnics or small gatherings in a family member's home or backyard. They have evolved into major events (3–5 days) with 50–1000 family members in hotels, on cruises, or other venues depending upon the economic ability and desire of the family group. Travel opportunities for black people opened up after the passage of civil rights legislation in the 1960s. By the 1970s and 1980s blacks felt welcome in hotels and restaurants. African American family reunions now account for half of all family reunions. Black family reunions represent a major economic force—it is estimated that 70 percent of nonbusiness travel by African Americans during the summer is reunion related.[2]

Family reunions promote family values by telling and retelling the stories of struggle and perseverance of the family unit; displaying unconditional love of family members; focusing on areas that are important to the family such as education or religion; and demonstrating respect for elders and other behaviors, which hopefully are adopted by the younger generations.

The level of sophistication in the organizing and functioning of family reunions varies significantly. Some families operate on an informal basis while others have formal officers and directors who are responsible for communicating with family members; managing funds (for instance, scholarships for family members and investment of funds); and managing the passage of traditions and rituals through the family reunion experience.

Family Reunion Case Study

The Chavers family of Tennessee provides an example of a family which has solidified its traditions regarding building its family history; helping others; and retaining ownership of their land through family reunions.

A Philanthropic Covenant with Black America

In July of 1972 Kissiah and Nicholas Chavers would have celebrated their 100th wedding anniversary. The occasion was celebrated by the descendants of their twelve children who held the first of several family reunions (the most recent being 2006) on the family farm in Mt. Pleasant, Tennessee. Four grand-daughters, two living in Chicago and two in Nashville, planned the 1972 reunion to meet new family members, renew family ties, share family stories and history, and visit the family farm. The Chavers family descendants had migrated to Chicago, St. Louis, and Cleveland, primarily, although several members still lived on the family farm.

The granddaughters (third generation) of Kissiah and Nicholas enlisted their husbands and children to plan and finance the first reunion. The location, Nashville, Tennessee, was chosen because of its proximity to the family farm, which was only 30 miles away. The reunion was a tremendous success attracting over 120 people from all over the country.

Family members held a business meeting and decided to hold a Chavers Family Reunion every five years, on a week-end, during the month of August. A planning committee was selected with representatives from the four major cities where family members lived (Chicago, Nashville, Cleveland, and St. Louis). Although there are always discussions about changing the venue, Nashville has remained the location for all of the re-unions because the most popular activity has been the visit to the family farm. The original home built in 1830 is no longer stand-ing. Only the chimney remains and family members who lived in homes on the farm have moved away. However, the family cemetery remains an active burial ground for family members and ownership of the 143 acres of farmland and 84 acres of woodland still remains in the family.

Reunion weekends always begin Thursday night with a welcome party for the early arrivals. On Friday morning chartered buses take the family to the Mt. Pleasant farm where a solemn ceremony is held in the family cemetery in memory of the ancestors. The history of the homestead is related by the elders, and the strong of heart sip a drink of sulfur water from the well. The rest of the day is spent roaming the farmland; enjoying a large picnic; posing for family photos and, finally, a trip into the small town of Mt. Pleasant for a visit to one or two shops and the ice cream parlor. The day ends with a long nap on the bus ride back to Nashville.

On Saturday morning family history is shared with family members and new additions are added to the family tree, which is maintained and updated by one family member who designed an elaborate family tree reflecting each of the twelve second-generation branches. She brings the document to each reunion and family members add new births and deaths.

Saturdays also include seminars by family members on various topics such as auto maintenance, investments, and crafts. A business meeting is held to discuss finances and to determine who will be responsible for the next reunion. To finance the reunions a small registration fee is assessed each family, and donations and sponsorships are solicited from those family members who are able to make the commitment. The afternoon is usually free time, and in the evening a banquet dinner with live music is held. The reunion ends Sunday morning with a farewell breakfast.

Within the Chavers reunion format, several traditions have been started and nurtured:

Building the Family History. Starting with oral history, Chavers family members have progressed to serious research and documentation of family genealogy and history. A fourth-generation cousin wrote her Masters thesis in history based on her research of the Chavers family. Perhaps the most important item she discovered was the last will and testament of Nicholas J. Chavers' father, Jones Daley, a white land owner in Maury County TN. The document substantiated family stories that Jones Daley left $418\frac{1}{2}$ acres to Nicholas (identified as a mulatto child living in the household). Family members continue to add photos and documentation to the family history.

Retaining the Land. The Chavers family has never lost sight of the good fortune of having received an inheritance of land. Nicholas Chavers specified his desire in writing that should the land be sold, it is to be offered *first* to family members. His wish has been respected since the 1850s. Fifth- and sixth-generation family members whose only connection to the farm has been through their visits during reunions have become purchasers of parcels of land as they become available. Reunions have helped to instill meaning and energy toward the commitment of keeping the land in the family.

Helping Others. Fundraising efforts within the Chavers family have been directed toward offsetting the cost of the reunions so that all family members can attend. In addition, parents and grandparents are encouraged to assist their children and grandchildren by underwriting some of their costs associated with attending the reunions.

Visits to the cemetery led to conversations about perpetual maintenance of the grounds. A family member designed an annual assessment, which would be given, voluntarily, by family members. However, notices are sent to family members each year. The family is also pursuing a means of providing ongoing funding for maintaining the grounds, cleaning the headstones, and other general maintenance.

Within the last few years younger family members have taken a more active role in soliciting the support of the family for charitable contributions. Their efforts have yielded support for marathons supporting cancer research as well as other charitable events. A sixth-generation family member has established a fund for elder care in his community in the name of his grandmother. Family members have begun to contribute to this memorial fund.

Giving Circles

According to Wikipedia, "Giving Circles" are a form of philanthropy consisting of groups of individuals who pool their funds and other resources to donate to their communities and seek to increase their awareness and engagement in the process of giving. Members of giving circles donate their own money or time to a pooled fund, decide together where to give these away, and often have some sort of social or educational interaction associated with the giving. Many circles, in addition to donating their money, also contribute their time and skills to supporting local causes. Donations may range from spare change to thousands of dollars each year. Women continue to make up the majority of today's giving circles—but the make up of circles is more diverse with respect to race, age, and gender.

Charitable giving is strongly imbedded in our country's culture. Mutual aid societies, fraternal orders, lodges, volunteer organizations, fundraising campaigns, foundations and individual contributions are all part of the philanthropic landscape—all having served the purpose of helping others in need at various periods of our country's history. According to philanthropy scholar and former president of the Council on Foundations, James A. Joseph, "the bulk of giving, more than 80 percent, comes from individuals. Collective or shared giving, while never absent from American life, is more prevalent in the public consciousness due in part to the growing visibility of giving circles."[3]

Giving Circle Case Study

The 2007 annual report of the Renaissance Women (RW) of Chicago, Illinois, noted that since 1978 they have given over $100,000 to African American organizations and individuals to fulfill their mission "dedicated to the rebirth of consciousness and improving the future of African American people."

The Renaissance Women is a group of Black women who came together in 1978 to express their dedication to the future of black people by giving financial contributions, writing, speaking, and organizing events that influence decisions and decision makers on behalf of black people. Renaissance Women represent many backgrounds, professions, and interests.

Six women remain from the original 17 who formed the group. At this time members range in age from mid-thirties to mid-sixties with incomes from lower to upper income; they are single, married, and divorced; some are mothers of elementary school children, others are grandmothers; all are formally educated—most with college degrees, some with graduate degrees.

All RWs have leadership positions in professions, or fraternal and religious organizations. They have honed skills in the fields of management consulting, social service administration, business, media production, government, sales, financial services, education, law, and medicine. They have many common goals, but they also benefit from their differences. The glue that binds them is a social consciousness that has led them to being involved in giving their time, expertise, and financial support to other black people and organizations so as to improve the overall quality of life.

RWs are proud of their history and the fact that they have shared information with hundreds of people on topics ranging from AIDS to the struggle against apartheid in South Africa. Symposiums which were held from 1981 through 2003 (see list at the end of this chapter) were replaced by other forms of outreach such as breakfast meetings with small groups and varying forms of written communications such as letters and position statements to newspaper editors and political leaders. RWs have contributed time and dollars to over 70 local and national black organizations, programs, and individuals. They targeted their dollars over 10 broad categories: arts and culture; education; employment and training; family support organizations; health care; public policy; senior citizens; support for women, children and others in need; and child care organizations.

The RW founders were young women who had recently completed their college educations and were employed in at least one job. They enjoyed some measure of financial security (which meant they had enough money to pay the rent and provide the next two meals.) Therefore, they were able to think about the needs of others. They felt an obligation to give something back to the black community. They were ready for the influence of their mentor, a diminutive woman with a will of steel named Dr. Effie O. Ellis.

Dr. Effie O. Ellis (June 15, 1913 to July 5, 1994) was an African American pediatrician who advocated for the "quality of life concept," which called for the integration of six aspects of life including: intellectual, social, physical, economic, spiritual/ethical, and mental/emotional. This was breakthrough thinking in the medical field in 1970. In addition, she was the first in many areas:

- First African American woman graduate from University of Illinois Medical School
- Served on Sergeant Shriver's Task Force, which developed the Head Start model
- Accompanied Richard Nixon on the first visit to China for an American president
- Headed the AMA as the first African American Executive Director
- Promoted comprehensive services for children by providing consultation with the March of Dimes and the City of Chicago

Dr. Ellis was a highly respected, dedicated, unrelenting advocate for children and their mothers. Therefore, when she approached a small group of impressionable young women they were awed and motivated to follow her lead to be of service to their community. She identified young women with "potential", introduced them to each other, encouraged them, and helped them to believe that they could change the world.

Beginning with their earliest meetings in 1979 there was chemistry between them, which is generated by energetic young people who are anxious to eradicate injustice, poverty and ignorance. A quote from early minutes states, "We were in absolute agreement on our mission; however, we struggled with defining the vehicle for our actions. Should we provide direct service, or advocacy, or both? Should we focus on fundraising and if so, how? Should we work through the political system—partisan or nonpartisan?" They debated such issues for months. In fact the intensity and length of that discussion caused some early RW members to leave the organization. But resolution and definition of the RW action plan gradually emerged.

The RWs decided to focus on "advocacy" rather than direct service. Rather than fundraising, they agreed to donate their own money to causes. They established monthly dues to support the activities of the group. Initially, they opted out of focusing on the electoral political process, either partisan or nonpartisan, in order to avoid dissension derived from strongly felt differences in ideology. As the members bonded over the years they became comfortable discussing their political views.

The membership of the group is limited to 20 people; the number of people who could be accommodated easily within each member's home.

Over the past 28 years, over 60 women have been members of the Renaissance Women. Reasons for joining the group were similar to those of the original members. Reasons for leaving RW ranged from geographical moves, changed priorities, death, and life changes.

They are frequently asked, "What keeps RW together and focused on an intangible purpose such as improving the future of black people?" One reason for their continued existence is the respect they have for each other's thoughts and opinions. They support each other. A contingent of the Renaissance Women is always there when a member is experiencing the good times and the bad times. The promotions, birthday parties, public appearances, important civic occasions, hospital visits, and funerals are attended by RW sisters. In addition to their mission they are a support group for each other. But they are not a "social group." They do not play cards, have dances or gather without discussing some aspect of their mission.

In 1982, the Renaissance Women began the process of identifying an "agenda" for black people. During their research they discovered that a Black Leadership Family Plan had been developed by the Congressional Black Caucus in 1971. Rather than reinvent the wheel, they decided to review the Plan and determine if it was applicable to their goals and objectives. The Midwest coordinator for the Plan was Harold Washington, congressman of the First Congressional District, state of Illinois.

They met with Congressman Washington, who readily supplied them with copies of the Plan which had a threefold purpose: to develop a basic set of rules by which black Americans could live; to establish a Black Development Fund; and to provide a set of instructions for implementation of the Plan. They decided to introduce the Plan to Chicago and planned a 1982 conference around that purpose. Congressman Washington agreed to participate in their program and engaged Congressman Walter Fauntroy, who represented Washington, D.C., to be their keynote speaker.

Their conference opened to a full auditorium of eager people. It was the first public appearance for Congressman Harold Washington after he had announced that he would run for Mayor of Chicago.

They presented the Black Leadership Family Plan and led a dynamic discussion on the instructions for implementation of the Plan and the Black Development Fund. They covered the following 12 rules for black unity, survival, and progress:

1. Support the Black Church
2. Protect the Elderly and Support Youth
3. Excel in Education
4. Oppose Crime
5. Contribute to the Black Development Fund
6. Buy and Bank Black
7. Register and Vote

8. Hold Your Elected Officials Accountable
9. Support Black Family and Community Life
10. Challenge and Boycott Negative Media and Support Positive Media
11. Secure and Defend the Black Community
12. Support Mother Africa and Caribbean Nations

A major component of the Black Leadership Family Plan was the Black Development Fund (BDF). It espoused a simple principle: support the agencies that support us. The Plan estimated that the combined income of the black community was nearly $150 billion per year. The Black Development Fund (BDF) postulated that "if 1% of our Black income was given to Black agencies and institutions, there would be a total of $1.5 billion a year given to African American self help efforts."

There were two underlying themes of the Black Development Fund. First, it promoted giving—a systematic way of giving support to black organizations and institutions. The black community through its religious institutions was familiar with the concept of tithing. The BDF was an extension of the principle. Secondly, the BDF provided a method of keeping more black income and black wealth in the black community.

The Black Development Fund stipulated that money should be given directly to organizations to support issues, interests, and organizations. It established categories of institutions, one for each month. The money would be sent directly to the institution. There was no middle man. It allowed the control of the giving to remain in the hands of the giver. The only requirement was that a letter was to accompany the contribution explaining that the contribution was part of the Black Development Fund movement.

Following are the categories for each month as specified in the Plan:

January	Black Civil Rights Organizations
February	Black Candidates, Black Political and Voter Participation Organizations
March	Black Religious Organizations
April	Black Senior Citizen Organizations
May	Black Africa and Caribbean Relief
June	Historical Black Colleges
July	Black Legal Defense Funds
August	Black Hospital and Health Care Organizations
September	Congressional Black Caucus (Political Action Committee)
October	Black Arts and Cultural Organizations
November	Black Family Support Organizations
December	Black Youth and Child Care Organizations

Their symposium attendees were energized; thoughts and ideas flowed; the conference was an unequivocal success. Participants were asked to sign a contract and commit to taking action toward following the Black Leadership Family Plan.

Congressman Washington listened to the audience and spoke to their issues and concerns. He offered recommendations and was candid in his criticism of institutions that had failed to respond to the issues. He did not campaign for the office of mayor at the conference, but his earnest support and participation won RWs respect and long-term loyalty. Thereafter many of the Renaissance women worked tirelessly to elect Congressman Harold Washington to be the first black mayor of the City of Chicago, in 1983 and 1987.

The Renaissance Women continued to support the Black Leadership Family Plan and held several conferences to spread the word and engage the black community in their mission.

Mayor Washington continued to endorse the goals outlined in the Plan and emphasized the need to focus on the Plan and not the man. He recognized that one man could make a difference, but one man, alone, could not sustain the mission. In reviewing the latter part of the 1980s and the decade beginning with 1990 it appeared that the black Community lost sight of the Plan. Mayor Washington died in November 1987. Affirmative action was under attack across the nation. Drugs, unemployment, and a failing education system assaulted the black community, leading to a sense of hopelessness and despair.

The Renaissance Women held fast to the principles of the Black Leadership Family Plan. They believed in supporting African American organizations and the methodology for giving. They consistently supported the Plan in two ways. They promoted the Black Development Fund in all of their programs and they adopted the BDF as their operating principle.

They encouraged all recipients of their donations to adopt the BDF and give to black organizations and institutions on a monthly basis. They have not been able to determine the full extent of their promotion of this principle. They have anecdotal evidence that other groups and individuals have bought into the practice. There are individuals who have said that because they were exposed to the concept they had given more and focused their giving on African American institutions.

At each monthly meeting of the Renaissance Women, they continue to select an organization using the categories previously identified to determine a recipient for a donation of funds. Each RW member pays a monthly sum, and the total amount is given to a black organization or institution. They started with $5.00 per person, per month and have increased the monthly, per person contribution to $35.00 per month.

Initially their BDF contribution was voluntary, but it is now mandatory, a condition of membership. Over the years they have made a number of adjustments to the process, but have maintained their commitment to the goal. For example, they renamed the BDF for their founder, Dr. Effie O. Ellis. It is now the Effie O. Ellis Award (EOE Award). They generally identify organizations related to family support, women, and children for each of the categories identified by the BDF. They have also experimented with the giving schedule. When their membership falls below the maximum number of 20, they award the EOE every other month to increase the amount of the contribution.

The Effie O. Ellis Award (BDF) is a standard agenda item at their monthly meetings. Each RW may nominate an organization to receive the monthly donation. The nominating member provides a description of the agency and the purpose for which the donation is to be given. A majority vote determines the recipient. Usually, they reach consensus on the recipient before a vote is taken.

They have also experimented with how nominees are identified. At one point Renaissance Women formed research teams to identify organizations that were qualified to receive their contributions in each of the Black Leadership Family Plan categories. Currently, they rely on each RW's expertise or interest to determine the nominees for the EOE award (BDF).

In prior years there was substantial discussion on what constitutes a "black organization." They debated whether or not to support an organization that was focused on helping black people but not controlled by black people. They finally adopted the following definition for "black organizations": the board of the organization must be at least 51 percent African American and the organization must serve a majority African American population.

There have been several occasions when they have given contributions outside of the EOE Award (BDF) to projects or organizations that do not meet the definition of black organizations. As an example, many of their members promote and solicit funds for Crossroads, a program supported by a group of physicians, devoted to raising funds to treat AIDS in African countries. Individual RW members contributed a day's wages to the fundraising campaign. Similarly, training programs directed toward a black audience organized by the YMCA in Chicago have received several individual donations from RW members outside of the EOE Award (BDF).

As they ended the year, 2007, they had donated over $100,000 to black organizations, institutions, and individuals. Their donations have been received as a statement of encouragement by some and have been viewed as a substantial financial grant by others. The EOE Award (BDF) has also become a way of supporting organizations in which RWs are members. They learn about each woman's involvement in other programs as well as what is going on in the community when they have their EOE Award (BDF) discussions. Whenever they have more than one nomination in a month, they usually decide to support the organization in which an RW member is involved.

In addition to supporting each other, the EOE Award (BDF) has been a method for supporting the speakers who give their time to their symposiums. It is not uncommon for RWs to donate to the same organizations year after year. Generally, the Renaissance Women support long-standing institutions and agencies, although they have given to new programs.

They find the majority population distancing themselves from the problems of African Americans and there is a growing chasm between black middle-class wage earners and blacks who are in the lower economic level. The Effie O. Ellis Award (BDF) remains the most tangible and accessible vehicle by which individuals can make a difference. RWs believe in the EOE Award (BDF); they will continue to support it; and they believe that their small efforts have made a difference. A quote from the Black Leadership Family Plan that the group finds particularly inspiring:

> *Our Leader died while we were on page three of the Plan. Now that the funeral is over, let us proceed to page four.*
> —Ossie Davis, June 18, 1971

Common Elements of African American Family Reunions and Giving Circles

While African American family reunions and giving circles may differ in several areas, such as organizational structure, function, and short-term goals, there are several commonalities.

Build Community. Family reunions strengthen and build the family by establishing and deepening family ties, sharing values, and providing a loving environment in which family members can thrive. Family stories and history that are passed from generation to generation nurture and strengthen the family structure by instilling and reinforcing values. These same qualities are evident in our case study of the Renaissance Women's giving circle. The Renaissance Women organization provides a safe environment for members—one where thoughts and ideas are accepted and sometimes criticized by supportive women. The members are professional women who have flourished in this supportive environment.

The sharing of financial resources in the Renaissance Women has allowed them to maximize their individual contributions so that they could have a stronger impact on the African American community.

Shared Learning. One of the benefits of giving circles is the learning associated with deciding which issues to address and identifying which organizations should receive the organization's contribution. By discussing the issues and the pros and cons of potential recipient organizations, RW members gain a better understanding of the problems and the ability to address them by community based resources.

As family reunions have evolved over the years they have expanded their role in providing family members with information on a range of topics. It is not unusual for family reunion agendas to include workshops on financial planning, family medical history, and healthy eating tips along with scrap booking and quilting tips.

Establishing Wealth. The Chavers family demonstrates how the purchase of land on the original homestead has become a part of the family's value system. Sixth-generation descendants have purchased tracts of the "original" land, which assures the transfer of the family legacy as well as an inheritance for future generations.

The Black Development Fund is a plan for creating wealth in the black community. The Renaissance Women giving circle embraced the *Plan* in an effort to support black institutions with dollars from black women. In addition, the Renaissance Women continue to promote this approach among other individuals and organizations.

Develop Leadership. The presence of a strong leader is a final common element in family reunions and giving circles. In both of the case studies, one or two individuals took responsibility for organizing the family reunion or identifying the group of women who started the RW giving circle. Leadership must be nurtured in order for it to grow and evolve over time.

Addendum Renaissance Women Symposiums

1981 **Our Children—Our Future**
1982 The Black Leadership Family Plan
1983 It's Not the Man—It's the Plan
1984 Crime in the Black Community
1985 Illinois Black Leadership Roundtable
1986 The Impact of the Media on Black People
1987 Public Education—Making It Work for Black People
1988 South Africa—Their Struggle Is Our Struggle
1989 Drugs, Teen Pregnancy, AIDS: The Black Church Responds
1990 One Person Can Make a Difference
1992 When and Where I Enter—Paula Giddings
1993 Health Care Reform
1994 Violence: Prevention and Solutions
1998 Sistahs Taking Voice For Ourselves
2001 Cycle of Domestic Violence
2002 Breast Cancer and the African American Female
2003 AIDS and the African American Community: Where Are We Now?
2003 Women's Financial Planning Workshop

Notes

1. Ione D. Vargus, "More Than a Picnic: African American Family Reunions." Working Paper No. 21, The Emory Center for Myth and Ritual in American Life, Temple University (2002).

2. Jennifer Crichton, "Family Reunion, Everything You Need to Know to Plan Unforgettable Get-Togethers" (1998).

3. www.givingforum.org (Forum of Regional Associations of Grantsmakers: Giving Circles in the Context of American Philanthropy) attributes statement to James A. Joseph, *Remaking America: How the Benevolent Traditions of Many Cultures Are Transforming Life* (San Francisco: Jossey-Bass, 1995).

Chapter 8

Time and Talent: Volunteerism as a Resource for Black Communities

Rodney M. Jackson
Founder and CEO, The National Center
for Black Philanthropy, Inc.

National Statistics and Trends

- Eighty-five percent of nonprofit agencies and 92 percent of congregations use volunteers.
- Forty-four percent of adults volunteer.
- Fifty-two percent of teens volunteer.
- Over the last five years the average number of people volunteering has increased, but the number of hours they volunteer and the frequency of their volunteer work has decreased.

(The preceding items are from the Independent Sector survey [2001], and the following items are from the Corporation for National and Community Service [2003].)

- National volunteer rate: 26.2 percent. Total volunteers: 60.8 million.
- National total hours volunteered: 8.1 billion.
- There were one million more volunteers in 2007 than 2002, and volunteering is stronger now than two decades ago.
- Over a third of volunteers serve intensively, volunteering 100 or more hours in a year.
- Data since 1989 show that religious organizations have consistently remained the most popular organizations for volunteers to serve through, followed closely in recent years by educational and youth organizations.
- Since 1989, the Midwest region of the United States has had the highest volunteer rate among U.S. regions for adults (32.2 percent), college students (31.8 percent), and baby boomers (31.8 percent).
- The South had the highest number of volunteers for 2007, with 20.8 million people who participated in service.
- The Northeast regional had the highest percentage of volunteers who chose to fundraise or sell items to raise money as their volunteer service (30 percent).

African Americans

- African Americans hold the second-highest percentage of volunteers in America: Whites volunteer at a higher rate (28.3 percent) than blacks (19.2 percent), Asians (18.5 percent), and Hispanics or Latinos (13.9 percent) (U.S. Department of Labor, 2006).

- African Americans are more likely to engage in volunteer activities sponsored by African American organizations because such organizations are more likely to solicit their support (Carson, 1998).
- Church involvement is associated with a greater likelihood that African American men will volunteer and that they will be members of a community-based organization. (Mattis et al., 2000).
- College students follow the national trend in volunteering, with females (33 percent) volunteering at a higher rate than males (26.8 percent), and whites (32 percent) volunteering at a higher rate than students of other races and ethnicities (23.6 percent). However, 39.2 percent of black college student volunteers engage in mentoring activities, compared to 22.3 percent of white college student volunteers (Corporation for National and Community Service, 2008).

Origin of Volunteerism in the African American Community

Volunteerism and philanthropy[1] have been integral parts of the African American community for nearly 200 years. For the majority of the history of Africans in America, there were few, if any, societal institutions established to look out for their general welfare. "Historically, black philanthropy," wrote Dr. Emmett D. Carson, "has been a survival mechanism through which African American people have directed their money, time and goods to lift up and advance the myriad interests of African American people."[2] It fell to African Americans themselves to look out for their own needs. As early as the late eighteenth century, African Americans began organizing Mutual Aid Societies and self-help organizations to provide a safety-net for widows, orphans, the sick, and others in need. The earliest of these self-help organizations were the Fraternal Order of Prince Hall Masons established in Boston, Massachusetts in 1775 and the Free African Society in Philadelphia, Pennsylvania in 1787. By the early 1800s, several hundred of these mutual-aid societies existed in many parts of the country.

Along with the simultaneous establishment of the Historically Black Churches,[3] these organizations began the great traditions of African American philanthropy and volunteerism that persist to this day. According to the Reverend Dr. Alicia D. Byrd, philanthropy included the donation of one's time as well as one's money. "After all," wrote Reverend Byrd, "if one does not have much money, then one's next most valuable possession is time and that, in many instances, can be almost as good as money."[4] But black volunteerism, like black philanthropy, had to be practiced in secret for many decades because, in many parts of the country, both were illegal. As a result, little is known about early volunteer practices among African Americans, although contemporary research by Dr. Emmett Carson and others is beginning to shedding greater light on this aspect of black history.

Contemporary Volunteerism among African Americans

Until recently, *black volunteerism*, like *black philanthropy*, was considered an oxymoron. The conventional wisdom seemed to be that "blacks don't volunteer," just as it used to be believed that "blacks don't give." While the research into volunteering in general is growing, there is a glaring dearth of research on African Americans and other communities of color, for that matter. Even two landmark studies on volunteering by the Corporation for National and Community Service—*Volunteering in America: 2007 State Trends and Rankings in Civil Life* and *Volunteering in America: 2007 City Trends and Rankings*—provide little information about racial or ethnic trends in volunteering.

The best research on black volunteerism may be contained in reports by the U.S. Department of Labor and in studies by nonprofit organizations such as the Independent Sector in Washington, DC, and the Centers on Philanthropy at Indiana University and the City University of New York. Even so, the primary focus of the university studies is volunteerism under the rubric of philanthropy. On the other hand, the Bureau of Labor Statistics reports include race. The Bureau reports that "Whites continued to volunteer at a higher rate (28.3 percent) than blacks (19.2 percent), Asians (18.5 percent) and Hispanics or Latinos, 13.9 percent."[5] This is actually good news for African Americans because the data show that they have the second-highest percentage of volunteers in America, more so than other nonwhites. (These data complement studies of African American philanthropy by the Independent Sector, the *Chronicle of Philanthropy*, and others that have found that African Americans give a higher percentage of their disposable income to charity than any other racial group in the United States, including whites.[6])

As we have shown, African Americans, contrary to popular opinion, give of both their time and their money. But the perception persists that the opposite is true. For organizations seeking to increase the number of African American volunteers, let's examine a statement by Dr. Carson in a paper he wrote for the Center for the Study of Philanthropy, City University of New York. "African Americans," wrote

Dr. Carson, "are more likely to engage in volunteer activities sponsored by African American organizations because such organizations are more likely to solicit their support."[7] The two most important elements of this quote are "activities sponsored by African American organizations" and "more likely to solicit their support."

Just as African American philanthropy had its origins as a survival mechanism for black people,[8] the same can be said of volunteerism. With no other established networks of social support, black people had to develop their own, so their philanthropy and volunteerism were first focused on basic survival. Then, as history progressed, the focus shifted gradually to education, civil rights, political involvement, and economic development. Although basic survival is no longer the focus of most African Americans today, all the other issues, to one degree or another, still remain pertinent. This is why "giving back" has been identified as one of the principal motivations for black philanthropy and, by extension, volunteerism, and why philanthropy that benefits the black community will continue to be important to African Americans.

Recruiting and Retaining African American Volunteers

The other important element of Dr. Carson's statement, that African American organizations are more likely to solicit the support of other African Americans, can be understood within the number one axiom of fundraising: *you must ask in order to receive.* Nothing gets drummed into the head of fundraisers more than "ask," "*ask,*" "*ASK.*" Even the Bible says to "Ask and it shall be given you."[9] People have to be asked to volunteer as well as give. There may be a variety of reasons that "Church involvement is associated with a greater likelihood that African American men will volunteer..." but one of them is surely that churches are not shy about asking; either to give or volunteer your time. If you are shy, hesitant or, perhaps, even afraid to ask African Americans to give and/or volunteer, *get over it,* because this is the only way it's going to happen.

Three studies validate the importance of asking: (1) a 2006 study conducted by Peter D. Hart Research Associates for Volunteer Match, "Volunteer Match User Study," identified the 10 most effective ways of recruiting volunteers. The top five were (i) word of mouth, (ii) Volunteer Match's website, (iii) Internet recruiting services, (iv) live presentations to groups, and (v) events;[10] (2) The Bureau of Labor Statistics reported that "about 43 percent of volunteers became involved after being asked,"[11] and (3) Independent Sector reported, "Individuals who were asked to volunteer were much more likely to volunteer (71 percent) than those who had not been asked (29 percent)."[12]

Once volunteers have been recruited, retaining them should be of paramount concern.

The key to retaining volunteers is employing good management practices. In a 2004 study of volunteer management conducted for the Urban Institute, the authors reported the results of a study conducted by the UPS Foundation that found "two-fifths of volunteers have stopped volunteering for an organization at some time because of one or more poor volunteer management practices."[13] The study identified eight management elements[14] that the authors said are essential to good volunteer management and retention:

1. Supervision and communication with volunteers
2. Liability coverage for volunteers

3. Screening and matching volunteers to jobs
4. Regular collection of information on volunteer involvement
5. Written policies and job descriptions for volunteers recognition activities
6. Annual measurement of volunteer impact
7. Training and professional development for volunteers
8. Training for paid staff in working with volunteers

The study authors hastily add that "not all practices can or should be adopted by all charities."[15]

The study also quotes Grossman and Furano who identified three elements they considered crucial to the success of any volunteer program:

1. "Screening potential volunteers to ensure appropriate placement in the organization,
2. Orientation and training to provide volunteers with the skills and outlook needed, and
3. Management and ongoing support of volunteers by paid staff to ensure that volunteer time is not wasted."[16]

Another key to good management practices was identified in the Corporation for National and Community Service's *Issue Brief: Volunteer Retention*: Volunteer retention is related to the type of organization where a person volunteers and to the activities that the volunteer performs.[17]

Finally, we asked one of our own volunteers, Ms. Penland L. Woods, an employee of the federal government, who has made an avocation of volunteering for several years for many different nonprofit organizations, what she felt from first-hand experience were the most important elements in managing and retaining volunteers. Ms. Woods listed the seven most important elements she considers when deciding on volunteer assignments:[18]

1. The environment must be safe and accessible.
2. The organization must be reputable and address an important community need.
3. Show appreciation for "free (but otherwise) billable hours."
4. It helps if volunteers don't have to pay for their own meals.
5. Recognize, graciously, that they chose you. Since volunteers also come with expectations, *exceed* them.
6. Attract people with an affinity to your cause.
7. The organizations must be reputable and the volunteer activity well organized.

Final Notes

In researching this chapter, I conducted searches on the Web's two biggest search engines, Google and Yahoo, to try to identify sites aimed at recruiting African American volunteers. While I found many organizational sites searching for African Americans volunteers for disease-related programs, foster parents, mentors, court-appointed special advocates, museum assistants, wild life conservationists, and so-forth, I did not find a single site that functioned as a national clearing house for African Americans such as Volunteer Match, Volunteer.org, and U.S.A. Freedom Corp. that recruit from the general public, including African Americans. I believe such a site would be helpful in increasing the number of African Americans volunteers, and by cross-linking with the aforementioned sites, it would make African Americans more aware of the vast volunteer opportunities that exist and expand the recruiting options for the vast array of organizations that use these other sites to recruit.

There is no better way to conclude this essay on volunteerism than by recalling the words of Dr. Martin Luther King: "Everybody can be great, because everybody can serve."

A Sample of Successful Volunteer Programs

Big Brothers Big Sisters of Eastern Missouri, St. Louis, MO

Big Brothers Big Sisters of Eastern Missouri reports that it[19] has successfully recruited over 340 African American volunteers to mentor youth throughout the St. Louis region, making this the agency's most successful recruitment effort in history. Today, one in every three calls to the agency is from African American volunteers. "Our organization has become extremely proactive in reaching and retaining African-American volunteers," said John Suggs, director of community engagement for Big Brothers Big Sisters of Eastern Missouri. "We've tried many strategies, but the most successful one has been simply caring about the community we serve." Big Brothers Big Sisters of Eastern Missouri is the oldest, largest and most effective youth mentoring organization in the State of Missouri.[20]

The Black Philanthropic Alliance, Washington, DC

The Black Philanthropic Alliance (BPA) is the first local membership organization of its kind for black professionals working in or supporting philanthropy in the Greater Washington, DC region. Its mission is to increase the presence and leadership of black professionals in philanthropy, and to increase black participation, giving and leadership throughout the local nonprofit sector. Its website is www.blackphilanthropicalliance.org.

National Association for the Prevention of Starvation, Huntsville, AL

The National Association for the Prevention of Starvation (NAPS) is a 501(c)3 nonprofit volunteer relief organization founded in 1978 in Alabama. Its mission is to mitigate hunger, poverty, and disease, and to improve education and food security among suffering people, both nationally and internationally, regardless of race, religion, or nationality. The organization provides humanitarian aid and educational support in the areas of emergency relief, skilled volunteers, health care professionals, agricultural technology, and social and spiritual comfort. The organization operates independently of all governmental, institutional, or political influences.

NAPS is an early response team as demonstrated in recent disasters such as crisis in Sudan, New York on 9/11, the tsunami in Sri Lanka, hurricanes, floods, and tornados. The organization brings rapid relief and comfort to those in despair. Children are the focal point of our services. In addition to our social services, NAPS is very active in HIV/AIDS and violence prevention and food security for the most vulnerable. The organization has offices in Guyana, Ethiopia, Jamaica, Madagascar, Sudan, and Zambia.

NAPS can be visited at www.napsoc.org. It was also featured in *The Covenant in Action,* www.covenantwithblackamerica.com.

National Center for Black Philanthropy, Inc.

Hands-On Philanthropy Day
In 2005, the National Center introduced a unique volunteer program for people attending its National Conference on Black Philanthropy. Hands-on Philanthropy Day—an opportunity

to volunteer or give—was launched at the Fifth National Conference in Minneapolis, Minnesota. On the day before the conference opened, nearly 40 volunteers from among conference attendees worked at six nonprofit organizations in the Minneapolis-St. Paul area. Volunteers did everything from reading to children, to helping in a food kitchen, to assisting with a large special event.

One year later, at the Sixth National Conference held last June in Washington, DC, conferees volunteered at four agencies in the DC area, preparing food, packing clothes, stocking food pantries, sorting donations, replenishing clothing racks, and going out on boats to clean up trash along the river's shoreline. This tradition will continue when the Seventh National Conference opens on March 29, 2009—in New Orleans, Louisiana.

Programs on the Drawing Board

The National Center has two ideas for volunteer programs in different stages of development. The more advanced of the two, Business Partners for Children and Families, seeks to match African American business owners and entrepreneurs with agencies, disadvantaged children, and families. The program was developed with support from the W.K. Kellogg Foundation and the Annie E. Casey Foundation. The second is the Volunteer Village, a temporary residence for volunteers responding to large-scale disasters.

Helping communities rebuild after natural disasters takes a considerable amount of time. One of the biggest problems for volunteers in such situations is finding low-cost housing, transportation, and meals. This was particularly the case in New Orleans where vast acreages of housing, including hotels and college dormitories, were wiped out, severely limiting available housing even for those who were on someone's payroll, much less those who weren't. Enter the Volunteer Village.

The original idea, in the early aftermath to Katrina, was to put unused FEMA trailers to good use by asking FEMA to donate 20 or so to form the basic units of housing for the Volunteer Village. The trailers were to have been placed on land the use of which its owner had already agreed to, free of charge. (At some point a private school was going to be built on the land.) Then the National Center was going to approach major corporations and state and local government to donate materiel that would have linked the trailers into a little neighborhood complete with electricity, running water, sewage, Internet, and, of course, security to ensure the safety of the volunteers. A hotel chain was going to be asked to operate it at minimal cost to guests, and major food chains were going to be asked to contribute discount food coupons. There could have been an "official airline" providing discount airfares, and local vendors providing discount transportation to project sites.

Then Murphy's Law intervened, and the Center learned, along with the rest of the nation, that FEMA trailers were hazardous to your health. With no suitable alternative at the time, the idea was abandoned.

However, we still believe the basic concept of the Volunteer Village—using donated materials and building on donated public or private land and utilizing volunteer time from public and private sources to mold the area into a temporary, functional community—has the potential for solving at least some of the temporary housing problems for volunteers. The concept is also applicable to refurbishing existing buildings adjacent to disaster areas that could have long-term or permanent use.

We also recognize that the U.S. economy will have to recover significantly, if these ideas are to have a snowball's

chance in Hades of being realized. Visit our website at www
.blackphilanthropy.org.

Tavis Smiley

Tavis Smiley Leadership Institute

The 2008 Leadership Institute, conducted by the Tavis Smiley
Foundation, took place August 14 through 18 on the campus
of UCLA in Los Angeles. More than 200 students who were
chosen based upon academic achievement, a letter of recom-
mendation, leadership and community service and an essay, participated in the event. Since its inception more than 5,000 youth
ages 13 to 18 have participated in the foundation's leadership
training workshops and conferences. Many teens in the program
have entered and completed college, organized health fairs and
voter registration drivers, conducted teen town hall meetings,
started businesses, and interned with city mayors and presidential
candidates.

The mission of the Tavis Smiley Foundation is to enlighten,
encourage, and empower youth by providing leadership skills
that will promote the quality of life for themselves, their communities, and our world.

SOBU Builds in New Orleans

In November 2007 Tavis Smiley announced that his Annual
State of the Black Union (SOBU) symposium, in addition to
examining the role African Americans would play in presidential elections, would also mobilize 1,000 volunteers to rebuild
some of the poorest areas devastated by Hurricane Katrina.
SOBU Builds opened on Friday, February 22, 2008, with about
1,200 volunteers working in six community service projects. See
www.tavistalks.com.

Volunteer Opportunities of Note

Disaster Initiative

Partnering with FEMA and the National Voluntary Organization Active in Disaster (VOAD), the Points of Light Foundation & Volunteer Center National Network is the lead organization in the management of unaffiliated volunteers in disasters. Much of the long-term recovery occurring within many communities postdisaster is conducted using trained volunteers. To learn how you can get connected to an organization in need of volunteers, please go to www.helpindisaster.org. To learn about volunteer opportunities in your community, please go to www.1800volunteer.org. Is your volunteer center responding to a local disaster? If so, please provide them with the information that can be posted here. E-mail dsmith@ PointsofLight.org.

Dr. Martin Luther King Day of Service

January 19. Initiated by Congress in 1994, King Day of Service builds on Dr. King's belief in community service by transforming the federal holiday honoring Dr. King into a national day of community service grounded in his teachings of nonviolence and social justice. With thousands of projects planned across the country, the 2009 King Day of Service on January 19 may be the biggest and best ever!

Building homes, delivering meals, refurbishing schools, reading to children, signing up mentors and much, much more, over 500,000 Americans honored Dr. Martin Luther King, Jr. by serving on January 21, 2008. The King Holiday engages four million Americans in service each year through Senior Corps, AmeriCorps, and Learn and Serve America.

HandsOn Network

HandsOn Network. Generated by Points of Light Institute. Affiliates, also known as Volunteer Centers, HandsOn Action Centers or Cares organizations, are the engine through which HandsOn Network connects thousands of volunteers to meaningful service opportunities throughout the United States, and increasingly, throughout the world. Affiliates work on a community-wide basis across various issues to develop high-impact volunteer programming. Through building relationships with nonprofit, school, faith-based, corporate partners, and others, affiliates play a critical role in leveraging volunteer power to the fullest effect. Affiliates implement programming in a wide variety of ways, shaping their work according to the assets and needs of their local communities.

National Philanthropy Day

More than 50,000 people across North America celebrated the twenty-second anniversary of National Philanthropy Day throughout November 2008 as a way of reminding the public about the importance of giving and volunteering, especially during difficult economic times. National Philanthropy Day (officially recognized on November 15) is coordinated by the Association of Fundraising Professionals (AFP) and pays tribute to the extraordinary contributions that charitable giving and volunteerism have made to society. AFP celebrates National Philanthropy Day through more than 100 events across North America where local donors, volunteers, foundations, businesses, young people, and others are honored for their charitable work. www.afpnet.org.

National Volunteer Week

April 19–25, 2009 and April 18–24, 2010. National Volunteer Week began in 1974 when President Richard Nixon signed an executive order establishing the week as an annual celebration of volunteering. Since then, every U.S. president has signed a proclamation promoting National Volunteer Week. Additionally, governors, mayors, and other elected officials make public statements and sign proclamations in support of National Volunteer Week.

During National Volunteer Week, organizations of all types host awards ceremonies recognizing millions of our nation's volunteers for their outstanding contributions to their communities over the past year. Simultaneously taking place during National Volunteer Week, thousands of volunteers also participate in local community service projects.

Your organization can also become certified to present the President's Volunteer Service Award to deserving volunteers during National Volunteer Week, as well as throughout the year. The President's Council on Service and Civic Participation sponsors this top volunteering award.

For additional information about National Volunteer Week, please contact Pat Chandler at (404) 979–2920 or pchandler@handsonnetwork.org.

Notes

1. As used in this volume, philanthropy includes the donation of one's time and abilities as well as money.
2. Emmett D. Carson, Ph.D., "African American Philanthropy at the Crossroads," *Proceedings of the First National Conference on Black Philanthropy* (Washington, DC: The National Center for Black Philanthropy, Inc., 1998), 2.

3. For a discussion of the development of the historically Black Churches and their relationship to the Mutual Aid Societies, see C. Eric Lincoln, Ph.D., "Philanthropy in the Black Church: the First 100 Years," *Proceedings of the First National Conference on Black Philanthropy* (Washington, DC: The National Center for Black Philanthropy, Inc., 1998).

4. Alicia D. Byrd, Rev. and Ph.D., *Philanthropy and the Black Church, Volume I* (Washington, DC: The Black Church Project, Council on Foundations, 1989).

5. U.S. Department of Labor, Bureau of Labor Statistics, "Volunteering in the United States, 2006."

6. Michael Anft and Harvey Lipman, "How Americans Give: Chronicle Study Finds Race Is a Powerful Influence," *Chronicle of Philanthropy* (2003).

7. Emmett D. Carson, Ph.D., "Black Volunteers as Givers and Fundraisers," paper prepared for the Center for the Study of Philanthropy, Conference on Volunteers and Fundraisers (New York: City University of New York, 1990).

8. Emmett D. Carson, Ph.D., "African American Philanthropy at the Crossroads," 2.

9. Matthew 7:7, King James version.

10. Peter D. Hart Research Associates, "Volunteer Match User Study: Findings for Quantitative and Qualitative Opinion Research Conducted June to August 2006 for Volunteer Match," p. 8.

11. U.S. Department of Labor, Bureau of Labor Statistics, "Volunteering in the United States 2006."

12. Independent Sector, "Giving and Volunteering in the United States 2001."

13. Mark A. Hager and Jeffrey L. Brudney, "Volunteer Management and Practices and Retention of Volunteers," Urban Institute, June 2004.

14. Ibid.

15. Ibid.

16. Ibid.

17. "Issue Brief: Volunteer Retention," Corporation for National and Community Service (2007).

18. "A Guide to Volunteering in Community Service," Penland L. Woods (August 2007).

19. Parenthesis mine.

20. From Big Brothers Big Sisters of Eastern Missouri, www.bbbs.org (St. Louis, MO, November 2008).

References

Anft, Michael, and Harvey Lipman. 2003. How Americans give: Chronicle study finds race is a powerful influence. *Chronicle of Philanthropy*.

Byrd, Alicia D., Reverend and Ph.D. 1989. *Philanthropy and the black church, Volume I*. Washington, DC: The Black Church Project, Council on Foundations.

Carson, Emmett D., Ph.D. 1998. African American philanthropy at the crossroads. *Proceedings of the First National Conference on Black Philanthropy*. Washington, DC: The National Center for Black Philanthropy, Inc.

———. 1990. "Black volunteers as givers and fundraisers," paper prepared for the Center for the Study of Philanthropy, Conference on Volunteers and Fundraisers. New York: City University of New York.

Corporation for National and Community Service. 2007. Issue brief: Volunteer retention.

———. 2008. Research brief: Volunteering in America research highlights. Washington, DC, July.

Hager, Mark A., and Jeffrey L. Brudney. 2004. Volunteer management and practices and retention of volunteers. Urban Institute, June.

Independent Sector. Giving and volunteering in the United States 2001.

———. 2001. Volunteering & giving. Washington, DC.

Lincoln, C. Eric, Ph.D. 1998. Philanthropy in the black church: The first 100 years. *Proceedings of the First National Conference on Black Philanthropy*. Washington, DC: The National Center for Black Philanthropy, Inc.

Mattis, Jacqueline S., Robert J. Jagers, Carrie A. Hatcher, G. Dawn Lawhon, Eleanor J. Murphy, and Yohance F. Murray. 2000. Religiosity, volunteerism, and community involvement among African

American men: An exploratory analysis. *Journal of Community Psychology* 28, no. 4 (June).

Peter D. Hart Research Associates. Volunteer match user study: Findings for quantitative and qualitative opinion research conducted June to August 2006 for Volunteer Match.

U.S. Department of Labor, Bureau of Labor Statistics. 2006. Volunteering in the United States.

Woods, Penland L. 2007. A guide to volunteering in community service. August.

Chapter 9

A Philanthropic Covenant with Black America

Rodney M. Jackson
*President and CEO, The National Center
for Black Philanthropy, Inc.*

This Covenant is a roadmap toward a plan of action to address the primary concerns of Black America today: from health to housing, from crime to criminal justice, from education to economic parity. Although these issues are often political, The Covenant itself is not strictly about politics. In fact, the words "Democrat" and "Republican" don't even appear in the text. The words that do appear include progress—hope—change—mission—purpose—family—neighborhood—love. You see, "We can't lead the people if we don't love the people, and we can't save the people if we won't serve the people."
—Tavis Smiley, "Opening Remarks,"
State of the Black Union 2006

The Covenant with Black America

The "Covenant" referred to above is the 2006 *New York Times* best-seller, *The Covenant with Black America*,[1] published by Third World Press, the first book by a black publisher ever to reach the *New York Times* best-seller list. *The Covenant*, as it is usually called, is a well-documented compilation of 10 major social and economic problems that still bedevil significant portions of black communities. From health care to criminal justice to economics to the so-called digital divide, not only did *The Covenant* describe these issues with unblinking and compelling efficiency, it also presented a series of bold strategies for addressing them as well. The 10 areas covered in *The Covenant* are:

1. Health and Well-Being: Securing the right to health care and well being
2. Education: Establishing a system of public education in which all children achieve at high levels and reach their full potential
3. Criminal Justice: Correcting the system of unequal justice
4. Police accountability: Fostering accountable community-centered policing
5. Affordable neighborhoods: Ensuring broad access to affordable neighborhoods that connect to opportunity
6. Voting: Claiming our democracy
7. Rural development: Strengthening our rural roots
8. Economic prosperity: Accessing good jobs, wealth, and economic prosperity
9. Environmental justice: Ensuring environmental justice for all
10. Digital divide: Closing the racial digital divide[2]

Achieving such lofty goals would be considered daunting at any time, but in the midst of the worst economic crisis since the Great Depression, one could be excused for considering these goals no more than impossible dreams. But if the election of Barack Obama as the forty-fourth president of the United States and the first African American to hold that office has taught us anything, it is that there are no impossible dreams. Conventional wisdom would have predicted that a young, virtually unknown, Midwestern senator, who had not yet served a full term, who was the son of an African man and a white American woman and whose middle name was Hussein, could not possibly win the U.S. presidency. As the entire world knows, not only was conventional wisdom proven wrong, but President Barack Hussein Obama was also elected in a virtual landslide, having raised more money and recruited more volunteers than any of his presumed deeper-pocket rivals. "Yes we can" became a never to be forgotten, "Yes we did."[3]

And who will forget the indelible image of President-Elect Obama walking to the podium in front of more than 125,000 cheering supporters in Chicago's Grant Park? Nor did it go unnoticed that the faces that greeted him that night were male and female, young and old, black and white, Asian American, Latino, Native American and everything in between. Such a multiracial, multiethnic, and, no doubt, mixed religious and mixed socioeconomic gathering brought back memories of similarly mixed coalitions that had walked side by side with Martin Luther King, that built schools to educate black children in the segregated South, that opposed slavery and built the underground railroad. All against impossible odds. All where "Yes we can" became "Yes we did." To get where *The Covenant* wants to take us, such coalitions will continue to play an important role.

A Philanthropic Covenant with Black America

The spirit of "Yes we can" must undergird any effort to solve the problems described in *The Covenant with Black America*, if the ghosts of inequities past, which still haunt black communities today, are to be exorcised. These problems are not new and Mr. Smiley's book is not the first to document them. But *The Covenant*, nonetheless, captured the American imagination in an unprecedented way and, as Tavis said, "presents a plan of action to address the primary concerns of Black America today." So, what, then, is the purpose of "A *Philanthropic* Covenant with Black America?"

First, *A Philanthropic Covenant* should be considered as a philosophical companion and complement to *The Covenant with Black America*. In one sense, the latter can be thought of as a "what" document; it tells *what* the problems are and suggests *what* solutions would be effective in solving them. The former can be considered a "how" document; its purpose being to show *how* certain resources—time, talent, and treasure—can be mobilized in new, strategic ways to impact black communities. Such resources are also known in modern parlance as *philanthropy*.

In the black community the concept of philanthropy is not well understood, and the word is infrequently used. Most African Americans would not usually refer to themselves as philanthropists. Philanthropy and philanthropists are thought to be people like the Oprah Winfrey, Bill Cosby, Bill Gates, and the Rockefellers. The word *philanthropy* is derived from a Greek word meaning "humane" or "benevolent."[4] In its broadest meaning, anyone who extends an act of kindness to someone else is performing an act of philanthropy. In its stricter sense, philanthropy may also be defined as "the exchange of goods and services from those with greater resources to those with lesser resources."[5] According to Dr. Emmett Carson, philanthropy, as it is typically practiced today, tends to be based on the European model of philanthropy—"top-down, donor-donee." But philanthropy in the black community, as in other ethnic communities, developed along a slightly different track.

During whatever period of American history one chooses, African Americans have always had less to sustain themselves and build for the future than their white counterparts. But that didn't stop blacks from sharing the little they had with those who had even less, such as widows and orphans. With a total absence of any state-sponsored safety nets until relative recently, blacks learned to look out for themselves and each other. Thus, an extensive network of Mutual Aid and Self-Help Societies[6] was formed in the eighteenth and nineteenth centuries to address social and economic needs that single individuals or families could not address by themselves. Blacks often shared what little money they had with those who had even less, and when there was no money at all, they gave of their time and their talent to help others. By any definition, these were true examples of philanthropy at its finest. This tradition of philanthropy, giving back or simply community service, can still be seen today in the giving and volunteer work of black fraternities and sororities, groups like 100 Black Men, the National Council of Negro Women, and many, many more.

Likewise, the rise of the historically black churches expanded these self-help networks while establishing the first historically black colleges and universities. Later still, black and white benevolence started the NAACP and the Urban League and helped the Civil Rights Movement as well. Today, African American philanthropy includes people whose philanthropy is based on both the European model and the more traditional mutual aid model. Examples of the former include well-known people like Winfrey and Cosby but also people who are not household names like Alphonse Fletcher, Eddie and Sylvia Brown, and Sylvia Johnson. Examples of the latter also include people like Matel Dawson, Oseola McCarty, and Maynard Jackson.

But one does not have to be a millionaire to be a philanthropist. In fact, Matel Dawson was just an ordinary man working on an assembly line in Detroit who decided to do something extraordinary with the little money he had. So the million dollars that he is estimated to have given away came from paycheck to paycheck, month after month, year after year. And Dawson was not the only one. Who can forget the remarkable generosity of Oseola McCarty, the black Mississippi laundrywoman who, having been denied admission to the University of Mississippi in the segregated South of her youth, nevertheless left Ol' Miss her life savings at her death so others would have the opportunity she was denied? The spirit of Matel Dawson and Oseola McCarty lives on in giving circles, donor-advised funds, and church tithing through which many African Americans have expressed their giving.

The primary purpose of *A Philanthropic Covenant with Black America* is to tap the rich tradition of African American philanthropy and self-help that has seen blacks overcome the worst of inequities to the point where an African American has become the forty-fourth president of the United States. *A Philanthropic Covenant* seeks to increase and channel that philanthropy in strategic directions to help overcome the remaining roster of evils that still suffocate too many black communities and rob America of the intellect, talent, and other contributions of too many black Americans. *A Philanthropic Covenant* is a broad invitation to everyone—grantmakers, individuals, families, professional fundraisers, churches, community organizations and youth—regardless of race, to enter into a new spirit of commitment, "Covenant Commitments," to improving black communities.

Covenant Commitments

Covenant Commitment may, at first, seem to be redundant; after all, a covenant is a commitment. In this case the word "Covenant" refers to *A Philanthropic Covenant*, and commitment is defined as a "pledge" or "binding contract."[7] Hence, a Covenant Commitment is a pledge or (self-imposed) contract to work for the improvement of conditions in black communities through the use of one's time and talents or the contribution of a portion of one's money or its equivalent (treasure). The following are examples of Covenant Commitments by:

- *Grantmakers*—providing additional funds through new grants or other donations.
- *Fundraisers*—helping small neighborhood-based organizations learn how to ask effectively for such funds.
- *Individuals*—becoming a mentor, a tutor, or a Big Brother or Sister; joining the neighborhood crime watch or eliminating environmental hazards.
- *Churches*—opening buildings and schools to community activities and engaging in planning efforts to mitigate the effects of natural disasters before they occur.
- *Families and groups*—encouraging the children to participate in community affairs and learn to be givers and not just recipients of them; forming Giving Circles and utilizing other resources within families to help other families.

- *Everyone*—becoming reacquainted with *The Covenant with Black America* and joining an issue that speaks to your passion.
- *Finally*—utilizing a website where you will be able to post and record your personal Covenant Commitments for all to see and, possibly, join.

The Covenant Fund

In addition to Covenant Commitments of Time and Talent, there is also a need for monetary contributions to ensure that sufficient funds are available to actually implement changes envisioned in the Philanthropic Covenant. We propose generating at least $100 million in new funding dedicated to improving black communities through a new gift vehicle to be known as the Covenant Fund. We have shown elsewhere in this book that funding for African American causes has been reduced over the past couple decades,[8] and the Covenant Fund is being proposed as one way of helping to assure that much-needed financial resources become available to address issues in black communities. As we envision the bulk of funding for the fund coming from African Americans themselves, traditional grantmakers could view such a fund as a strategic means of leveraging their own support by attracting new dollars.

The concept of a megafund to bolster black communities is not new. It was first raised by Dr. Emmett D. Carson at the First National on Black Philanthropy in March 1997. Before concluding his opening speech to the conference, Dr. Carson said:

> *Finally, we need to develop a national African-American Community Foundation. Its long-term goal should be to accumulate assets of $1 billion. Let me say that again—$1 billion. Such a goal*

is do-able and achievable if, and only if, it has the unconditional
support of the people in this room. Would it take two to three
decades or more of time-consuming, tedious fits and starts? Yes.
Would it be controversial? Certainly. Is it needed to help ensure
the now-threatened survival and advancement of future generations?
Absolutely, without any doubt.[9]

In describing the role of such a foundation, Dr. Carson said,
"Such an entity would ensure that African-American institutions that were judged essential to community survival . . . would
have the support to take unpopular stands, to monitor and bring
attention to issues and groups that are detrimental to our safety,
and to preserve our art and culture in all its forms."[10] He concluded his speech by saying, "We have the intellectual firepower
to create such an institution and run it effectively. We have the
collective resources to raise the capital and the know-how to
invest it. The only question is—do we have the collective will
to do it? I think and hope we do."[11]

Even if the financial boom of the last decade, prior to the
current economic meltdown, had continued, as Dr. Carson said,
building such a fund would have taken decades. In light of the
current economy, it appears that it may take lifetimes. (Of course,
$1 billion is a mere fraction of the money recently doled out
by federal government to the financial institutions, auto makers,
insurance companies, and so on.) So we are proposing the more
modest goal of $100 million, just 14 percent of the total raised
by President Obama during his campaign, as a down payment
on the ultimate goal.

We propose two ways of contributing to the fund. First,
one can contribute to the fund directly, a process to which we
will return in a minute. Second, one can choose to contribute
directly to any organization, church, religious institution, school,

college, fraternity, sorority, giving circles, donor-advised fund, or foundation of the donor's choice, as long as said entity is working to fulfill goals set out in *The Covenant with Black America* or *A Philanthropic Covenant with Black America*. In other words, we do not want the Covenant Fund to divert resources from established charities that are already doing good work in black communities. On the contrary, we want to see such funds expanded. When such gifts are made in the name of the Covenants, they will be credited to the Covenant Fund. One need only inform the fund that a gift has been made, and when verified, it will be added to the Covenant Fund total.

Second, for donors who would like their gifts to be used more strategically, they may contribute directly to the Covenant Fund itself. Unless otherwise specified by the donor, contributions made to the fund will be endowed so that such funds will be available in perpetuity to fulfill the goals of the Covenants. This means that the Covenant Fund must become an institution in its own right with a separate and independent board of directors, staff, bylaws, resource development, and funding strategies. We also propose that a role equivalent to an Inspector General within federal agencies be created and incorporated into the fund as an additional guarantor of the fund's honesty and integrity.

As previously stated, it is not the purpose of the Covenant Fund to replace or divert funding that otherwise be available to black communities. That would defeat its purpose. The point of the fund is to generate *new* money and use it strategically to invest in black communities. It is anticipated that fund resources could be used to support activities traditional funders try to avoid . . . like *capacity building* for nonprofit organizations. We hear the lament, all too frequently, from traditional funders that it is difficult to fund black organizations because they "lack capacity." Yet, the same funders infrequently help build that capacity, and when they do, it is often at a dollar level that doesn't do the job. Hence, the vicious circle: We can't fund them because they lack capacity, but they lack capacity because we won't fund them. However, such details concerning the actual structure and function of the fund must be left to another place and time.

Conclusion

There is no question that the election of the first African American as president of the United States is a watershed moment not just in U.S. history but in world history. While we should all take pride in and celebrate this signature accomplishment, we must not make the mistake of declaring, "Mission Accomplished," or feeling our work is done and we can now sit back and relax. Every time another black youth kills another black youth, we know our job isn't done. Every time we hear about failing kids in failing schools, we know our work is not done. Every time we hear that another black male has been incarcerated, we know our work is not done. Whatever positive things we are doing in our communities, we need to do more of them. Whatever we give, let's try to give a little more. However much we work, let's put in one more hour. We *are* the people we've been waiting for. For the sake of those we must not leave behind, "Yes we can" becomes, "Yes we must."

> *Everybody has something to give. No gift is too great or too small. Give as the Lord has blessed you.*
>
> —Rev. Dr. Cynthia Hale[12]

Summary of Chapter Covenants

Chapter 1 Empowering the African American Community through Strategic Grantmaking

Angela Glover Blackwell

Foundations spend billions of dollars a year to help solve the problems facing our country. By making a firm commitment to inclusion, foundations can ensure that their massive investment empowers African Americans and other communities of color and brings new strengths to the tough challenges that face us all.

- Significantly expand the racial diversity on the boards of foundations and recruit more people of color who have demonstrated a deep commitment to and knowledge of historically excluded communities. Turning to search firms that developed the walkabouts and skills to reach deep into these networks will improve the chances of success.
- Use grantmaking—issue-based as well as core funding—to strengthen institutions that serve the interests of people of color and to support and groom leaders of color. These investments pay off in unanticipated ways. For example, PolicyLink (the organization I lead, which has a diverse staff and board and works on a variety of issues that advance equity for all low-income communities and people of color, including African Americans), built a broad portfolio of policy expertise and a network of policy experts with generous core foundation support. PolicyLink was able to use these assets to make a valuable contribution to the black community when Tavis Smiley invited the organization to coordinate the *Covenant with Black America* book.
- Use a variety of institution-building investments: provide grants that help organizations build their communications

capacity; strengthen their fundraising skills; improve management performance; engage in broad coalitions; build partnerships with entities that bring different skills, such as research institutions; and enable organizations to quickly move to new opportunities by having some flexible resources.

- Demonstrate commitment to inclusion from the start by assembling diverse advisors to develop funding strategies. Hire consultants to do early assessments on the impacts of the issue area on different communities of color.

- Introduce organizations led by people of color to other funders; stay connected with these organizations and leaders by visiting their offices and developing supportive relationships. Highlight these organizations in publications, on websites, and in presentations. These activities help build the leadership and visibility of groups that often work heroically but invisibly in their communities.

- Invest in a pipeline of experts of color in foundation issue areas by funding appropriate professors and departments at historically black colleges and universities and by establishing fellowships that increase diversity in academic institutions generally. Consider loan forgiveness programs, mentorships, and other activities that build a cadre of experts of color who can enter fields that lack diversity, especially policy.

- Evaluate foundation program officers based on criteria that reflect the foundation desire to be more inclusive and build the capacity, visibility, and effectiveness of organizations that are accountable to communities of color and led by committed leaders of color.

Although it's important to focus on results, take time to broaden the universe of actors. Take risks.

Chapter 2 Philanthropy and Religion

Harold Dean Trulear

In light of the traditions and changes within the giving patterns of African Americans and their religious institutions, one can posit the following challenges and recommendations for present and future work:

- African Americans must resist the growing trend for their giving to houses of worship to be spent increasingly on institutional maintenance. The more that percentage grows, the less money flows outside the congregation to other noteworthy causes and institutions outside of the congregation.

- African American religious leaders must revisit their philosophy and theology of giving, wresting it from the self-interested notions of the contemporary prosperity movement and cultivating a sense and spirit of altruism, generosity, and philanthropy. Prosperity is not the enemy; prosperity for prosperity's sake is the culprit.

- African American congregations must hold leadership accountable, both locally and denominationally, to see that dollars pass through congregations to larger efforts such as missions, education, social agencies, and the like. To the extent that these dollars are diverted to institutional maintenance (for instance, keeping the denomination going or its leadership prosperous), they minimize potential support for historic institutions such as HBCUs (especially those still maintaining connection to houses of worship), health care and social welfare, and advocacy institutions such as the NAACP, the Urban League, the YMCA and others.

- The struggles and even closings of HBCUs begun and operated by historically black churches offend the memory of those congregations and denominations that birthed and nurtured them through their infancy. Religious giving to colleges at the denominational, congregational, and individual level must increase if the black community is serious about educational opportunities for the marginalized of our community.

- African Americans must financially support small to midsize congregations that provide the type of social capital and networks that strengthen neighborhoods and communities.

- The philanthropic community must grow in its recognition of the social value of religious institutions, and develop even more ways of supporting this work.

- Also, there exist two competing philosophies of giving that clash both within religious institutions, and in the tensions between the larger philanthropic world and religion itself. Simply put, this is the tension between quantity and quality of services. Religious institutions must resist attempts to sacrifice quality for quantity in the attempt to chase external support for their efforts.

- Returning to religious institutions for a word of summation, we press religious institutions to recapture their prophetic voice as champions of those oppressed, distressed and marginalized by social, cultural, and racial arrangements. While some would argue that recent efforts to provide government support for religious social services has muted the prophetic voice of black religion, others point to a waning prophetic voice in years prior to the promotion of faith-based initiatives. Gayraud Wilmore's pointing to the late-nineteenth- and early-twentieth-century "Dechristianization of Black Radicalism" and the "Deradicalization of the Black Church," the rise and subsequent decline of religious support for civil rights issues, and the entrenchment of the modern self-interested prosperity movement prior to government interest in supporting faith-based institutions all point beyond external forces culpable for the weakening of the prophetic. Ultimately, African Americans and their houses of worship must determine whether or not the prophetic voice is inherent to their religious traditions, or if it only flourishes when their own interests are the beneficiaries of prophetic witness. If to be religious one must be prophetic—then religious giving will reflect such a champion's spirit. If not, expect to see more and more of religious giving remain within the walls (figuratively and literally) of our houses of worship.

Chapter 3 Fundraising to Strengthen Black Communities

Birgit Smith Burton

Nonprofits need to ensure that their own fundraisers are educated, informed, prepared, and credentialed to address the particular nuances of the black community and the cultural dimensions that impact giving.

- **Develop a Better Understanding of African Americans as Donors.** In transitioning from traditional church and community-based giving practices, African American donors are particularly concerned with the impact of their money. Remember the report on African American giving produced by the Community Foundation of Greater Atlanta. "African American philanthropists hold themselves to high levels of responsibility to ensure meaningful contributions, or 'giving well.' Nonprofit organizations would do well to assist the African American to 'cultivate the philanthropist within' by addressing the issues of responsible giving."

- **If You Fail to Plan, You Plan to Fail.** Regardless of the color of the donor or the organization, it is essential to develop at least a basic fundraising plan in order to position yourself for success.

- **Ask for Help.** There are many opportunities in your community to obtain low-cost or even free assistance for your organization's fundraising. Such assistance can come from local or national consulting firms that may offer pro bono assistance to nonprofit organizations, local foundations that offer technical assistance with grant procurement or that support hiring a fundraising staff of consultants, nonprofit organizations like the Alliance for Nonprofit Management, and professional associations of individuals and organizations devoted to improving the management and governance capacity of nonprofits. The latter would include groups like the Georgia Center for Nonprofits and the Association of Fundraising Professionals.

- **Develop Innovative Ways to Raise Money.** Having planned, strategized, and organized your fundraising approach, it is now time to think of new and innovative ways to reach your audience. Following are some examples:
  - **Build Strategic Alliances.** Sometimes a merger between organizations with common objectives can have tremendous success. Pooling resources can raise an organization's visibility, increase its effectiveness, and attract support for its cause. Planning a successful alliance is critical. The following eight steps will help:
  1. **Start Small.** Start with an event or workshop with one partner. After you've gained experience you can team up with two or more partners at a time.
  2. **Identify Potential Partners.** Make a list of potential partners. Look for those whose missions are

compatible. Don't automatically pick an organization you already know well.

3. **Create a Statement of Purpose.** Explain why your organization wants to form an alliance in terms of your individual organization. *The more in harmony your organization is with your partner the more successful your partnership will be.*

4. **Jointly Establish Short-Term Goals.** Create measurable and attainable concrete goals.

5. **Be Sensitive to Each Organization's Long-Term Goals.** Each organization should know what the other organization's long-term goals are and respect them.

6. **Identify Responsibilities.** Clearly outline each organization's responsibilities.

7. **Define How to Resolve Conflicts.** Form a small committee from both organizations. This committee will oversee the alliance's operation.

8. **Build on Success.** Any nonprofit can find areas in which pooling resources makes sense. Joint efforts will help your organization, your partner's, and the entire nonprofit sector.

- **Motivate People to Form Giving Circles.** This is a form of philanthropy consisting of groups of individuals who pool their funds and other resources to donate to their communities and seek to increase their awareness and engagement in the process of giving. Convincing people to form Giving Circles involves many of the same skills used in other forms of fundraising.

- **Ask Fundraising Professionals to Donate Their Time.** Volunteer in your organization. Members of groups, such as the Development Assistance Project, often pool their talents and resources to assist organizations in their community with budgets under $1 million.

African American fundraisers must be willing to lend a hand as volunteers in organizations serving black communities.

- **When Our Nonprofits are Successful, Our Community Benefits.** Healthy nonprofit organizations continue to be fundamental to our achievement and progress as a black community. Our organizations inspire potential donors because of their mission, but remember that potential donors need more than that to be moved to give; effective fundraising is a critical element of that success.

Chapter 4 Youth in Philanthropy

Jeanette M. Davis-Loeb

How will philanthropists inspire members of the next generation to embrace the call to serve, and ensure that they have the knowledge, skills, and right attitudes to do so strategically and effectively? Here are ways to help facilitate that eventuality by teaching, modeling, and creating opportunities for black children to discover and harness the power of philanthropy.

- **Educate.** Young people have to learn about philanthropy and its critical role in our communities and our society. That means getting the subject of philanthropy into the schools, into after-school programs, youth-serving organizations and even religious classes.
- **Model.** National organizations have to take the lead in making a commitment to involve young people in their

philanthropic work. Once the commitment has been made, they must develop specific programs and resources that can be delivered to state or local chapters, and embark on an ongoing effort to encourage local chapters to involve youth as volunteers in their programs, as donors and fundraisers, and as participants in their governance.

- **Facilitate.** Young people have to be given opportunities to take on their own projects and experience what it means to make a difference.

- **Nurture and Support Our Youth.** Some say the greatest gift of any community is its ability to nurture and support its youth. Well, if that is the case, we have well and truly fallen down on the job, and it is time for us to get right back up. Historically, *philanthropy* is nothing new in the black community. More often than not, it has been the word itself and defining it by the standards of others that has caused some confusion for our folks. So it's not even that we don't know what to do; we're just not doing it; at least not in a way that touches the lives of almost everyone; particularly the lives of all our kids.

- **Take Care of Our Own.** Through common acts of kindness and sustaining our local institutions we've been giving and loving each other for centuries. Baking cakes to raise money for the church, feeding strangers and raising barns are just a few of the many acts of service we've bestowed upon one another. Honestly, had it not been for our propensity to take care of our own, we probably wouldn't have survived as a people for this long. So tell me, whatever happened to "what's mine is yours" and serving strangers as if they were family or close friends? When did we forget that you and me, we, were the community, and start looking to outside sources to fix what was ailing our communal body from within?

- **Don't Lose Another Child.** We are at a pivotal place in time where we simply don't have another child to lose, especially not another black boy. It's time we take back our power, people, and do what's right for each other. How many more of our children are we going to throw away, because we are too tired or because we expect to be given everything? What in the world! It is truly time to take our lives, families, and communities back.

- **Give to Receive.** When is the last time you volunteered at your church, spent some time at a nursing home on loving some of our elders, or even watched a neighbor's kid until a parent got home from work? When did we stop building each other up? When did we stop giving to receive? We don't have time to wait around for some organization to do the things that we can do for ourselves. That is too much like waiting for your captor to save you, and of that surely we've had enough. Our community organizations are there to help structure our combined activities and efforts, not to play mammy to some spoon-fed kids.

- **Lead by Example** and become a volunteer, especially parents.

- **Ask and Expect** our young people to join us in serving.

- **Mentor** in your community. Teach and model good stewardship.

- **Create** age- and skill-appropriate opportunities for young people to give.

- **Empower** our next generation of leaders to be the change.

Chapter 5 Civic Engagement in the African American Community

Stephanie Robinson and Charisse Carney-Nunes

The philanthropic community is already beginning to acknowledge the importance of civic engagement as a fundamental strategy in philanthropy. Without active and engaged citizens, the charitable goals of nongovernmental organizations will not be realized, and noble works of such organizations will be in want. The philanthropic community is best positioned to design a multipoint program to tackle the issues set forth in the Covenant. The points of the program relating to civic engagement are summarized above in our introductory essay. The proposed action steps for getting it done are summarized here.

What the Philanthropic Community Can Do

- **Step One: Define a "Community for Progressive Ideas."** The first step is to determine the identity of the members of the philanthropic community who will participate in the Philanthropic Covenant. Are we speaking of large foundations and community foundations? Does the community include smaller foundations, individual philanthropists and giving circles? What about corporations and governmental officials and policy makers?

- **Step Two: Convene the Community.** Build the bonds. Do the members of the community have shared values? Is civic engagement fundamental to philanthropy in their view? We suggest the community-building technique called "story sharing," in which a trained facilitator leads participants to share their experiences with each other. The subject matter of the circle would be to share our unique experiences with philanthropy. What projects work; what projects don't work, and why. We would seek to understand the extent to which citizen participation may influence a project's success.

- **Step Three: Reconvene the Community.** Trust, affirmation, mutual understanding, and deep commitment are necessary ingredients to the success of this community-building exercise. Therefore, the story-sharing and convening should be repeated at least twice before any agenda-setting is attempted.

- **Step Four: Agree on Process.** The community must agree on a process for setting priorities.

- **Step Five: Action.** The community is finally ready to define an action plan and funding strategy to make real their progressive agenda and ideas. The plan would likely include an analysis to lead to more strategic grantmaking in the progressive ideas sector; a funding strategy for grassroots philanthropy; and a funding strategy for civic engagement and democratic practice. The plan would also include a coordinated support strategy that would train the next generation of progressive thinkers and activists; build an infrastructure of think tanks and advocacy groups; invest in media and media transparency; fund legal organizations; support religious organizations; and create working networks of philanthropic institutions.

What the Community Organizations and Local Faith Communities Can Do

Many individuals and organizations within and outside our community are already working very hard on each of the Covenant-agenda items. The overall purpose of this good work is to make life better for our communities. Many of these organizations are woefully under-resourced—both in terms of cash and human resources. As organizations seek to increase the effectiveness of their efforts, the challenge is often grounded in resources, and the harsh reality is that if such organizations do not greatly multiply and increase their financial and human resources, they will fail. Here are some steps that community organizations, including faith-based organizations, can take to increase their effectiveness in this regard:

- Recognize the importance of strategic planning and capacity building. Raise funds specifically for this effort as you solicit donations and seek funding.
- Register your organization with Volunteer Match: www.volunteermatch.org.
- Write and implement a raising strategy.

What Every Individual Can Do Now

Former President Bill Clinton's latest book entitled, *Giving*, provides an excellent framework around which individual citizens can have in impact in philanthropy. These strategies demonstrate that every gift matters, and that you don't have to give a Buffett-sized gift to make a difference.

- **Read *Giving*.** Pay special attention to the stories collected about everyday citizens and the difference that they have made in the world. These stories are inspiring, and as we read about the actions of others, we are better able to imagine our own capacity for real change.

- **Give Money.**
  - You do not have to be a billionaire. Your giving should be proportional to your income. Tithing is one of the oldest traditions in Black America. Try to set aside at least 10 percent of your income for charity. If you cannot handle 10 percent, pick another percentage, and stick to it. One of the stories Clinton tells in his book is about two Minnesota sixth graders who set a goal of collecting

only $1 from each of their peers to contribute to Katrina relief. When all was said and done, their modest goal setting turned into a $24,000 gift to the victims of the hurricane.

- Join or form a Giving Circle. A giving circle is a group of donors who place their charitable dollars into a pooled fund, and decide as a group which charities to support. They can vary in size, structure, and charitable focus. Giving circles have exploded as an innovative way that ordinary Americans can have an enormous impact in philanthropy. A recent study estimates that giving circles have raised about $88 million since 2000 and show no signs of slowing down. The 10 basic steps to forming a giving circle are available on the website of the Forum of Regional Associations of Grantmakers at www.givingforum.org.

- Encourage others to give. Network with your family and friends. Let them know about the organizations and ideas that you find interesting and important. Remind them of their moral obligation to give back to their religious institution, community organization, or school. Black colleges have endowments and alumni giving rates that are among the lowest in the nation.

- **Give Time.** While we may not all have access to money, everyone has access to 168 hours each and every week. Sometimes the gift of time can be more rewarding and long-lasting than money. Visit www.VolunteerMatch.org to locate volunteer organizations near you. Volunteer opportunities include mentoring, tutoring, lending professional skills, home building, life-skills/financial skills coaching, and even story sharing. In his book, President Clinton recounts the volunteer work of a 22-year-old young woman in Lesotho,

Africa, and the impact she was having on hundreds, simply by sharing her story. Volunteerism is one of the most important indicators of civic health and participation in a democracy. Although people so often equate civic participation with merely voting or monetary contributions, our democracy simply could not thrive without *volunteerism*.

- **Give Things.** Most Americans are blessed with an over-abundance of things that we use to make our everyday lives more convenient. Individuals seeking to make a difference, and who want give more than just money should also consider donating useful items. The challenge is, of course, to donate items that are truly useful to people in need, rather than items of little or no value. *Giving* sets forth stories about several organizations that specialize in making this assessment. Doc to Dock is an organization that collects and delivers medical supplies and pharmaceuticals to health providers in Africa and the Middle East. The U.S.-Africa Children's Fellowship collects and donates educational materials, school supplies, toys, and games, and donates them to the Zimbabwe Organization of Rural Associations for Progress. Other useful items that can be collected and donated are bicycles, cars, furniture, construction supplies, musical instruments, and sports equipment. Items can even be auctioned on eBay with the proceeds going to charity.

- **Give Skills.** One of the most useful things that someone can give is a special skill. Skills in demand include tutoring, life-skills coaching, financial skills coaching, and professional skills such as lawyering or health care. Diverse professionals such as hair stylists, cosmetologists, engineers, social workers, and psychologists can find a great demand for their skills, depending on the particular situation. Be creative. Keep an open mind. And search out or create opportunities to volunteer whenever they arise.

Chapter 6 An African American Response to Natural Disasters

Sherece Y. West and Kermit "K.C." Burton

- African American leaders must be a voice for their communities in advocating for government policies and practices that outline the responsibilities of government to address disaster-impacted communities with enough funding and relief service supports to get the job done. They must be reliable and close to the ground to provide timely problem solving and decision making in cooperation with government officials and other stakeholders.
- Black institutions, particularly black churches, historically black colleges and universities, and other anchored institutions, can play an important role in addressing disaster readiness and rapid response. Faith-based organizations have demonstrated the ability (with Katrina and Rita) to act as frontline responders that can quickly mobilize their congregations to provide food, shelter, and relief. Black churches have been highly successful in amassing a significant level of relief funds and placing families with other out-of-state congregations.
- The black community must also make specific covenants for change with a variety of other sectors: health, banking and finance, legal, educational, media (including information and entertainment media), as well as personal and family support networks.

- The nonprofit sector, particularly black community-based organizations, can play an important role during disasters by helping to coordinate emergency services, provide support to individuals and families, and coordinate their efforts with black churches and other community stakeholders.

- For organized philanthropy, funding should be focused on investing in advocacy and supporting grass-roots leadership. Funding should also be flexible enough to provide for preparedness and rapid response and to build the capacity of anchored institutions so they can truly function as first responders.

- President Obama should re-establish the White House Interagency Task Force on Nonprofits and Government, which, during the Clinton Administration, collaborated with the Council on Foundations to make strategic investments in marginalized communities across the nation.

- A Black Philanthropic Covenant should include a commitment to support for wealth-building strategies. African Americans should covenant with the philanthropic sector to support black funds specifically created to respond to disasters and other crises. Such funds, at the Twenty-First Century Foundation (21CF) and Faith Partnerships Inc., provided important resources after Hurricane Katrina; the 21CF continues to serve as a credible contributor in the post-Katrina Gulf Coast.

- Finally, the black community should covenant with the philanthropic sector and other public and private funders to support better education for the general public regarding disaster/crisis readiness and response, including examining predisaster disaster/crisis vulnerabilities in many black communities.

Chapter 7 Families and Friends—The Power of Small Groups

Carol Brunson Day and Judith Gordon Samuel

While African American family reunions and giving circles may differ in several areas, such as organizational structure, function, and short-term goals, there are several commonalities.

- **Build Community.** Family reunions strengthen and build the family by establishing and deepening family ties, sharing values, and providing a loving environment in which family members can thrive. Family stories and history that are passed from generation to generation nurture and strengthen the family structure by instilling and reinforcing values. The Renaissance Women's (RW) organization provided a safe environment for members—one where thoughts and ideas are accepted and sometimes criticized by supportive women. The members were professional women who flourished in this supportive environment.

  The sharing of financial resources in the Renaissance Women allowed them to maximize their individual contributions so that they could have a stronger impact on the African American community.

- **Share Learning.** One of the benefits of giving circles is the learning associated with deciding which issues to address and identifying which organizations should receive the organization's contribution. By discussing the issues and the pros and cons of potential recipient organizations, RW members gain a better understanding of the problems and the ability to address them by community based resources.

  As family reunions have evolved over the years, they have expanded their role in providing family members with information on a range of topics. It is not unusual for family

209

reunion agendas to include workshops on financial planning, family medical history, and healthy eating tips along with scrap booking and quilting tips.

- **Establish Wealth.** The Chavers family demonstrates how the purchase of land on the original homestead became a part of the family's value system. Sixth-generation descendants purchased tracts of the "original" land, which assures the transfer of the family legacy as well as an inheritance for future generations.

  The Black Development Fund was a plan for creating wealth in the black community. The Renaissance Women's giving circle embraced the *Plan* in an effort to support black institutions with dollars from black women. In addition, the Renaissance Women continued to promote this approach among other individuals and organizations.

- **Develop Leadership.** The presence of a strong leader is a final common element in family reunions and giving circles. In both of the case studies, one or two individuals took responsibility for organizing the family reunion or identifying the group of women who started the RW giving circle. This leadership must be nurtured in order for it to continue to grow and evolve over time.

Chapter 8 Time and Talent: Volunteerism as a Resource for Black Communities

Rodney M. Jackson

What Government Can Do

- Reconvene the White House Conference on Philanthropy and include volunteerism and service as principal foci.
- Refocus on national service, and ensure that programs that promote volunteerism are fully funded.

- Test the concept of the "Volunteer Village" to determine whether such an approach to large-scale disasters is a feasible, cost-effective and efficient vehicle for providing volunteer help.
- Establish a national Internet website specifically to recruit African American volunteers and organizations that need their services. Such a site should be coordinated with other sites, such as the VolunteerMatch.org and the Points of Light Foundation, to provide additional opportunities for African American participation.

What Everyone Can Do

- Partner with black churches and other religious organizations in recruiting and utilizing African American volunteers.
- Review and put in place good management practices for recruiting and retaining black volunteers.
- Conduct additional research on volunteering by African Americans, paying particular attention to What Works.
- Black organizations that run national (or local conferences) should consider incorporating the concept of "Hands on Philanthropy Day" (or its equivalent) into conference programming as a way their conferences can have an additional positive impact on local black communities.

Notes

1. Tavis Smiley et al., *The Covenant with Black America* (Chicago: Third World Press, 2005).

2. For a quick review of the 10 Covenants, visit www.covenantwith blackamerica.com.

3. Visit www.barackobama.com.

4. *American Heritage College Dictionary*, 4th ed. (Boston and New York: Houghton Mifflin Company, 2002).

5. Rev. Alicia D. Byrd, Ph.D., "Philanthropic Activities of Black Churches: Celebrating the Past and Planning for the Future." In *At the Crossroads: The Proceedings of the First National Conference on Black Philanthropy*, ed. Rodney M. Jackson (Oakton, VA: The Corporation for Philanthropy, 1998), p. 31.

6. For a short but comprehensive history of African American philanthropy, see Dr. C. Eric Lincoln, "Philanthropy in the Black Church: The First 100 Years." In *At the Crossroads: The Proceedings of the First National Conference on Black Philanthropy*, ed. Rodney M. Jackson (Oakton, VA: The Corporation for Philanthropy, 1998), p. 13.

7. Ibid.

8. See also *Funding the New Majority: Philanthropic Investment in Minority-Led Nonprofits* (Berkeley: Greenlining Institute, 2008).

9. Emmett D. Carson, Ph.D., "African American Philanthropy at the Crossroads." In *At the Crossroads: The Proceedings of the First National Conference on Black Philanthropy*, ed. Rodney M. Jackson (Oakton, VA: The Corporation for Philanthropy, 1998), p. 10.

10. Ibid.

11. Ibid., p. 11.

12. Rev. Dr. Cynthia Hale, "Give and It will be Given to You." In *Black Philanthropy: From Words to Action*, ed. Dr. L. Lauretta Baugh (Washington, DC: The National Center for Black Philanthropy, Inc., 2005).

Reconciling King's Dream, Obama's Election, and the Imperative for a Black Philanthropic Covenant

Emmett D. Carson

The evolution of black philanthropy—the giving of money, time, and goods by African Americans—has been shaped, in large part, by the legal, social, and economic conditions that African Americans have faced over time.

The Imperative for a Black Philanthropic Covenant

When confronted with slavery, black philanthropy supported the Underground Railroad. When faced with Jim Crow, black philanthropy supported the Civil Rights movement. The charitable contributions of African Americans, often through their churches, created the first black schools, banks, and insurance companies. Whatever the challenge or opportunity, black philanthropy proved to be a consistent and reliable mechanism for collective efforts to secure the health and well-being of African Americans.

The election of Barack Obama as the 44th president of the United States raises profound questions about the relevance of a philanthropic covenant among African Americans. In one respect, Obama's election is tangible evidence that the last barrier in fulfilling the dream articulated by Martin Luther King, Jr. that African Americans would one day "not be judged by the color of their skin but by the content of their character" has arrived. There are very few remaining firsts for African Americans to achieve. We have had black lawyers, doctors, scientists, cabinet secretaries, mayors, governors, military generals, Fortune 500 CEOs, astronauts, foundation/nonprofit CEOs, entertainers, talk show hosts, television anchors, and now a president. By the yardstick of racial integration, individual African Americans have now broken through every job barrier.

While racism certainly continues to exist, it is difficult for anyone to argue in the wake of President Obama's landslide election that racism is the overriding determinant for whether an individual African American can succeed at his or her chosen endeavor. We should celebrate having reached this milestone even as we acknowledge that there is still unfinished work to be done in creating a fully color-blind society with zero tolerance for racism.

Viewed within this framework, some have begun to suggest that the next step in the evolution of black philanthropy is to see it as an individual activity rather than the collective enterprise that it has been historically. Individual African Americans would each make contributions and devote their time to causes that have personal meaning to them, but there would be little pooling of our resources to tackle shared interests and concerns. After all, having presumably achieved the goal of racial equality as evidenced by Obama's victory, each African American is now responsible for charting his or her individual destiny. I wholly reject this narrow interpretation of Dr. King's dream and the misinterpretation of what it implies for the future of black philanthropy.

The problem with this reasoning is that we have relied on one speech at a specific point and time—in this case, Dr. King's "I Have a Dream" speech—and have used it to define the entirety of Dr. King's thinking as well as to establish the sole benchmark for measuring African American progress. We are guilty of trapping Dr. King in time and thereby denying him any further growth in his ideas or his philosophy.

To understand the evolution of Dr. King's dream and decipher the real future of black philanthropy, we must move beyond his "I Have a Dream" speech of 1963 to his "Where Do We Go from Here?" speech of 1967. Let's quickly put 1967 in context. It is four years after the historic 1963 March on Washington. It is three years after the 1964 Civil Rights Act that provided public access and Dr. King's selection as a Nobel Peace Prize winner. It is two years after passage of the 1965 Voting Rights Act. It is a year before Dr. King's assassination, and he is well under way in planning for the Poor People's March on Washington.

Dr. King is 39 years old when he asks the question of himself and the movement: "Where Do We Go from Here?"

This is his answer:

"I want to say to you as I move to my conclusion, as we talk about 'Where do we go from here?,' that we honestly face the fact that the movement must address itself to the question of restructuring the whole of American society. There are forty million poor people here. And one day we must ask the question, "Why are there forty million poor people in America?" And when you begin to ask that question, you are raising questions about the economic system, about a broader distribution of wealth. When you ask that question, you begin to question the capitalistic economy. And I'm simply saying that more and more, we've got to begin to ask questions about the whole society. . . .

Now, when I say question the whole society, it means ultimately coming to see that the problem of racism, the problem of economic exploitation, and the problem of war are all tied together. These are the triple evils that are interrelated."

Dr. King saw the challenges of racism, economic exploitation, and war as separate but intertwined evils. Obama's victory speaks forcefully to the diminution of racism, but is meaningless as it relates to the issue of economic exploitation. So, how much progress have we made in achieving King's dream of economic equality? In describing the economic conditions of African Americans in the same speech, King observed:

"Of the good things in life, the Negro has approximately one half those of whites. Of the bad things of life, he has twice those of whites. Thus half of all Negroes live in substandard

housing. And Negroes have half the income of whites. When we view the negative experiences of life, the Negro has a double share. There are twice as many unemployed. The rate of infant mortality among Negroes is double that of whites. . . .

In other spheres, the figures are equally alarming. In elementary schools, Negroes lag one to three years behind whites. . . . One-twentieth as many Negroes as whites attend college. Of employed Negroes, seventy-five percent hold menial jobs. This is where we are."

Dr. King would be disappointed to see that when it comes to economic equality as opposed to political equality, sadly, we do not seem to have made much progress at all. Today, 42 years later, Dr. King's theorem that African Americans experience double the economic hardships of whites remains true. Consider these facts:

- We have reduced the number of those in poverty from 40 million to 36.5 million Americans.
- The poverty rate of African Americans is 24 percent compared to 8 percent for whites.
- The median household income of African Americans is 61 percent of whites, roughly $32,000 compared to $51,000.
- African American infants remain twice as likely as white infants to die before their first birthday.
- Black single parents are twice as likely as whites to live in low-quality housing.
- The unemployment rate of black males is 9.5 percent compared 4.0 percent for whites.
- Of 2 million people in prison, 44 percent are black.

- Fully 19 percent of African Americans, compared to 10 percent of whites, were without health insurance over a three-year period 2004 to 2006.

Dr. King's dream of economic equality remains unfulfilled. Unfortunately, despite individual successes, as a collective community African Americans have made no gains and, in some cases, are worse off than we were 40 years ago. In the areas of health, education, incarceration, housing, and environment, there has been virtually no progress in the collective well-being of African Americans. Our nation's singular focus on Dr. King's message of racial integration has obscured his later messages about economic injustice and war.

Assessed from this perspective, the need and the opportunity for a black philanthropic covenant have never been greater. The dawning of a postracial society means that there are more African Americans than ever who have the time, talent, and wealth to contribute in a collective effort to improve the socioeconomic status of African Americans. Now is the time for the collective philanthropy of African Americans to address Dr. King's forgotten dream of economic equality. The need for a black philanthropic covenant to address the economic ills of African Americans could not be more timely. The current economic crises will certainly exacerbate the difficulties already faced by too many of the poorest African Americans. Long-term, the globalization of the world economy will require that African Americans be fully prepared to compete in a twenty-first-century world that will reward education, innovation, and entrepreneurship.

The black philanthropic covenant envisioned in this volume can play an essential role of catalyzing and encouraging investment in the African American community by African Americans as well as others. While African Americans will and should always feel a unique social and cultural obligation to other African Americans, like President Obama's winning electoral coalition, African Americans must invite, welcome, and engage others to participate in the uplift of all African Americans. The United States will never reach and maintain its full potential in a world economy if there are significant segments of the population that are not prepared and able to participate. All Americans must be made to see that not only is it the right thing to do, but their own self-interest lies in making sure that all African Americans are fully productive taxpaying citizens, thereby fulfilling both King's economic dream as well as the American dream.

About The National Center for Black Philanthropy, Inc.

The National Center for Black Philanthropy, Inc. was established to promote and strengthen African American participation in all aspects of modern philanthropy. The National Center was incorporated in the District of Columbia on November 30, 1999, and received a determination in 2000 that it is tax exempt under Section 501(C)(3) of the Internal Revenue Code. The mission of the National Center is to promote giving and volunteerism among African Americans, foster full participation by African Americans in all aspects of philanthropy, educate the public about the contributions of black philanthropy, strengthen people and institutions engaged in black philanthropy, and research the benefits of black philanthropy to all Americans.

The National Center for Black Philanthropy, Inc.

The National Center conducts several programs, chief among which are national and regional conferences on black philanthropy that began in 1997 in Philadelphia, Pennsylvania, with the First National Conference on Black Philanthropy. In 1998, the first regional conference on black philanthropy was held in Minneapolis, Minnesota, in collaboration with several local organizations.

About the Editor

Rodney M. Jackson is the founder, President, and CEO of The National Center for Black Philanthropy, Inc. (NCBP) and founder of the National and Regional Conferences on Black Philanthropy. He previously worked in Washington, DC, as Director of Development for the Communications Consortium Media Center and as a consultant with the Milton S. Eisenhower Foundation and the National Council of Negro Women. Mr. Jackson also conducts workshops in fundraising and nonprofit management for organizations throughout the country under the auspices of the NCBP, the Support Centers of Massachusetts and New York, and the Grantsmanship Center among others. He also started and published the *Black Philanthropy* newsletter and has written articles for a variety of professional publications including the Proceedings of the National Conferences on Black Philanthropy, the National Black MBA Association Foundation, and Partners for Africa. Before moving to Washington, Mr. Jackson served as Director of Development for the African

About the Editor

American Institute in New York City, and before that, he held a variety of positions in both for-profit and nonprofit organizations in the Greater Boston Area. Mr. Jackson holds bachelor and masters' degrees from Boston College. He is married and the proud father of two adult children and three grandchildren ages six to nine.

About the Authors

Angela Glover Blackwell is founder and chief executive officer of PolicyLink, a national research and action institute that works collaboratively to develop and implement local, state, and federal policies to achieve economic and social equity. By Lifting Up What Works—using research to understand and demonstrate the possibilities for positive change—PolicyLink presents new and innovative solutions to old problems. PolicyLink is a leading advocate of equitable development, a comprehensive approach that includes the fair distribution of affordable housing throughout regions and equitable public investment. Angela is a co-author of *Searching for the Uncommon Common Ground: New Dimensions on Race in America* (New York: W.W. Norton, 2002), written with Manuel Pastor and Stewart Kwoh. She also collaborated with Tavis Smiley to develop *The Covenant with Black America*—a *New York Times* best-selling book of community and policy strategies for economic and social empowerment—and the follow-up *Covenant in Action*. She is a frequent guest in the media and her appearances include ABC's *Nightline*, *NOW* with Bill Moyers, and National Public Radio. She has been published in the opinion pages of the *New York Times*, the *Los Angeles Times*, and the *San Francisco Chronicle*; and has lectured widely on concentrated poverty and equitable development, appearing before audiences at the Chautauqua Institution and the Aspen Ideas Festival.

Birgit Smith Burton is Senior Director of Foundation Relations at Georgia Institute of Technology. With nearly 25 years of experience in the fundraising profession, Birgit began her career in Buffalo, New York, as Director of Public Relations for an ad agency managing special events including the local production of the Lou Rawls's Parade of Stars Telethon. This led to the United Negro College Fund's invitation to serve as the first area director for the Buffalo, New York campaign. Subsequently she joined the Office of Development at Georgia Tech and created the Arts Education Program uniting the Robert Ferst Center for the Arts at Georgia Tech with Centennial Place Elementary School. Birgit is a sought-after speaker on fundraising and development. The Council for the Advancement and Support of Education (CASE) recognized her as a "Faculty Star" for her national and international conference presentations. The Kresge Foundation selected her as an advancement expert to provide advice and counsel to participants in the Kresge HBCU Initiative. She also served on the Design Team for the Community Foundation for Greater Atlanta's study of African American philanthropy in metropolitan Atlanta. She is co-founder of the Southeastern Network of African Americans in Philanthropy (SNAAP), founder and chair of the African American Development Officers Network (AADO). Birgit currently sits on the boards of the A.E. Lowe Grice Memorial Scholarship Fund,

Hammonds House Galleries of African American Art, Robert Ferst Center for the Arts, the Founders Council of the National Visionary Leadership Project, Arts Leadership League of Georgia (ALL-GA), and Hosea Feed the Hungry and Homeless for which she currently serves as board chairman.

Kermit "K.C." Burton is Deputy Director of the Interfaith Center on Corporate Responsibility, a New York-based socially-responsible investing organization that through the lens of faith builds a more just and sustainable world by integrating social values into corporate and investor actions. From 1997 through 2008, KC was a Senior Associate of the Annie E. Casey Foundation, a private philanthropy where he shared a portfolio of work that included developing and implementing efforts at the foundation to encourage more of the philanthropic sector in America to direct a portion of their investments in place based ways to benefit disadvantaged children and families. That work included a focus African American and other ethnic philanthropy, faith-centered philanthropy, and grassroots community philanthropy. KC also managed the foundation's sponsorship and membership budgets. In 2005 after hurricanes Katrina and Rita struck the U.S. southern gulf coast, he was deployed for most of two years as a loaned executive to the Louisiana Disaster Recovery Foundation, concluding his last seven months as interim executive director. Afterward he continued to undertake a portion of the Annie E. Casey Foundation's work on philanthropic and community disaster readiness and response for vulnerable children and families. Initially at the foundation, he served for more than four years as Director of Baltimore Relations. Prior to joining the foundation, KC was the executive director of the Baltimore City Child First Authority, a legislatively created authority to establish after school learning centers in select Baltimore City schools. Prior to that, he was a public relations consultant and business owner for six years, following stints as public affairs manager and corporate responsibility manager for the *Baltimore Sun*, and positions in public and community relations for the Mayor's Office of Baltimore City, the Baltimore Symphony Orchestra, and the Maryland Department of Juvenile Services.

Charisse Carney-Nunes, writer, speaker and social entrepreneur, is the author of the children's books *I Am Barack Obama* (2009); *I Dream a World for You: A Covenant for Our Children* (2007); and *Nappy* (2006), as well as the book, *Songs of a Sistermom: Motherhood Poems* (2004). Charisse is a Senior Vice President of The Jamestown Project, an action-oriented think tank dedicated to making American democracy real. She is also the founder of Brand Nu Words, a company dedicated to publishing uniquely artistic books and related media that tell stories that too often remain untold. A graduate of Harvard Law School, Harvard Kennedy School of Government, and Lincoln University, Charisse's passion for instilling in children the lessons of history and their aspirations for tomorrow has become a consistent theme in her work. Charisse has served as a speaker or presenter for numerous national and regional organizations and schools. She has appeared on ABC News Now, Radio One, and American Urban Radio Networks.

Jeanette M. Davis-Loeb is the Founder and CEO of the Rising Oak Foundation, a national nonprofit organization committed to directly affecting the intellectual, psychological and spiritual development of boys of African descent. She is also the former V.P. and C.O.O. of Dynamic Industries L.L.C., specializing in property development and asset management. Over the past 15 years Jeanette has cultivated her commitment and passion to improving the quality of life in her community. At present she spends much of her time traveling the country, reintroducing our communities to the unique blessing, potential, and power of black boys. In addition to her work on behalf of boys of African descent, Jeanette is a board member and Resource Development Committee member of Women In Fatherhood, Inc., the outgoing chair of the Pacific Northwest Advisory Board of the United Negro College Fund, and the Founder/Chair of their "A Mind Is Annual Giving Society." She is also the author of *What Are You Bringing to the Party?— A Model for Success* (2009).

Carol Brunson Day is President and CEO of the National Black Child Development Institute whose mission is to improve and advance the quality of life of Black children and families through advocacy and education. For many years she served as CEO and President of the Council for Professional Recognition, home of the Child Development Associate National Credentialing Program and the National Head Start Fellowship Program. She has been a Reggio Emilia liaison, and currently serves on various national Boards, including the Anti-Defamation League's Miller Early Childhood Initiative, the T.E.A.C.H. Early Childhood Project, ZERO TO THREE Editorial Advisory Board, and Teach for America's Early Childhood Advisory Committee. She has authored more than 25 publications on diverse topics in early childhood, including professional development, multicultural education, and culture and child development.

Stephanie Robinson, Esq. is a nationally recognized social commentator and political analyst. She is an expert on issues relating to social policy, women, race, family, and electoral politics. Stephanie is the President and CEO of The Jamestown Project, a national think tank focusing on democracy, and is a Lecturer on Law at Harvard Law School. She is former Chief Counsel to Senator Edward M. Kennedy. Stephanie is a commentator on the *Tom Joyner Morning Show*, where she speaks to eight million people weekly offering her perspective on the day's most pressing social and political issues. She has been instrumental in her work with *The Covenant with Black America*—the *New York Times* best-selling book—and is the co-author, along with Tavis Smiley, of the third book in the series, *Accountable: Making America as Good as Its Promise* (February 2009). She also contributed to *The Covenant in Action*, the second *New York Times* best-selling book in the Covenant series. She was featured as one of the 30 Young Leaders of the Future in *Ebony* magazine and was profiled in the book *As I Am: Young African American Women in a Critical Age*, by Julian Okwu. Stephanie is a frequent speaker expressing her views in countless media outlets, including the Associated Press, the *Washington Post*, C-SPAN, and NPR.

Judith Gordon Samuel, a partner of Samuel Consulting, LLC, a firm that provides a range of human resources services including communication strategies, leadership development, employee relations, and organizational development, was formerly Vice President and Senior Human Resources Officer for CNA Insurance Company. Judith is a founding member and current president of Renaissance Women, an organization of African American women in Chicago who are committed to improving the quality of life of African American people through advocacy, research, dissemination of information, and directed action. In her spare time she is an artist, writer, and avid reader and studies genealogy. She is a member of the Afro-American Genealogical and Historical Society of Chicago and has researched one line of her ancestors through eight generations of American history. Judith is involved in several organizations and is on the board of the League of Black Women, the Landmarks Preservation Council of Illinois, and the YMCA Alliance of Chicago.

Harold Dean Trulear, Ph.D. is Associate Professor of Applied Theology at Howard University School of Divinity and a Fellow at the Center for Public Justice. Dean has worked as a consultant for the Annie E. Casey Foundation in their Faith and Families portfolio since 1998, and has also worked with a number of other philanthropic organizations, including the Ford Foundation, the Pew Charitable Trusts, the Cleveland Foundation, and the United Way of Massachusetts Bay in the development of their work with the faith community. He has taught religion, public policy, and community studies in several institutions, including Yale University, Drew University, Hartford Seminary, Gordon-Conwell Seminary, Fuller Seminary, and the Center for Urban Theological Studies. His research interests include religion and youth, juvenile justice, African American religion, and urban ministry. He is the author of several monographs including *Faith Based Institutions* and *High Risk Youth*, and *The African American Church and Welfare Reform*. Dean recently completed a three-year stint as vice president of faith-based initiatives at Public/Private Ventures, in Philadelphia, having come to P/PV from New York Theological Seminary, where he served six years as dean for first professional studies. He also coordinated several programs for high-risk youth with Youth For Christ/Campus Life in Paterson, NJ, and GLOBE Community Ministries in Philadelphia. He is a graduate of Morehouse College (BA) and Drew University (Ph.D.).

Sherece Y. West, Ph.D. is President of the Winthrop Rockefeller Foundation, and is nationally known for her leadership in the areas of community development, public policy, and, most recently, disaster recovery. Sherece's career path began at the Social Security Administration and wound its way through the Maryland Municipal League, the DC Department of Public Health, the Community Service Society in New York City, the Ford Foundation, and the Annie E. Casey Foundation. At Casey, Sherece partnered with its Rebuilding Communities Initiative grantees and consultants to help the five RCI sites advance their community-building plans and achieve their goals. It was her work at Casey that led the Carrier Foundation to invite Sherece to be its first President & CEO. Shortly after arriving there, Hurricanes Katrina and Rita struck, and after just two months on the job, Sherece was asked to help lead the Louisiana Disaster Recovery Foundation, first as a loaned executive and subsequently as its Chief Executive Officer. LDRF is committed to promoting equity and inclusion as communities build back in Louisiana, a mission that dovetails with the WRF vision of Arkansas as a state where economic, racial, and social justice is universally valued and practiced. In addition to heading WRF, she currently serves on the board of the Council on Foundations. Sherece was a 2007 Telly Award Bronze Winner for her work as Executive Producer of Power in the People. She holds a Doctor of Philosophy in Public Policy from the University of Maryland, Baltimore County; a Master of Public Policy from the University of Michigan Gerald R. Ford School of Public Policy; and a Bachelor of Arts from Bowie State University. She was a Fellow with the Alfred P. Sloan Foundation Policy Institutes and a 2003–2004 Emerging Leaders Fellow—a joint program of Duke University and the University of Cape Town in South Africa.

Index

Index

Index

Index

Index

Index